Francis and Clare
in poetry

An Anthology

EDITED BY
JANET McCANN
and
DAVID CRAIG

ST. ANTHONY MESSENGER PRESS
Cincinnati, Ohio

Cover and book design by Mark Sullivan

Library of Congress Cataloging-in-Publication Data

Francis and Clare in poetry : an anthology / edited by David Craig and Janet McCann.
   p. cm.
  Includes index.
  ISBN 0-86716-635-5 (pbk. : alk. paper)
  1. Francis, of Assisi, Saint, 1182-1226—Poetry. 2. Clare, of Assisi, Saint, 1194-1253—
Poetry. I. Craig, David, 1951- II. McCann, Janet.

PN6110.F74F73 2005
808.81'9382700922—dc22

                      2005010957

ISBN 0-86716-635-5

Published by St. Anthony Messenger Press
28 W. Liberty St.
Cincinnati, OH 45202
www.americancatholic.org

Printed in the United States of America

Printed on acid-free paper

05 06 07 08 09 5 4 3 2 1

CONTENTS

When he thought of God and saw the marvelous creations of God's overflowing love, Saint Francis would pick up a stick from the ground and draw it like a violin bow over his left arm. Then he would break into song, praising God in French, the language of his mother and of the troubadours he'd heard at the fairs of Champagne when he accompanied his father on cloth-buying trips. Blessed Thomas of Celano, Saint Francis' first biographer, himself a poet who wrote the apocalyptic medieval poem, "Dies Irae," writes of Saint Francis that he

> ...praised the Artist in every one of his works; whatever he found in things made, he referred to their Maker. He rejoiced in all the works of the Lord's hands, and with joyful vision saw into the reason and cause that gave them life. In beautiful things he came to know Beauty itself. To him all things were good. They cried out to him, 'The One who made us is infinitely good.' By tracing God's footprints in things Francis followed the Beloved wherever he led. He made from created things a ladder to God's throne.[1]

The ladder Francis made he often sang of, because he considered himself God's troubadour. He embraced his Lady as a Knight of the Round Table would embrace his Lady of the castle; only Francis' Lady was Gospel Poverty, which he dubbed Lady Poverty, serving her unselfishly and with the devotion of a Knight, the eloquence of a Troubadour. Like King Arthur's Knights and the Paladins of Charlemagne, Francis tested his spiritual prowess and devotion to the Lady Poverty by venturing into the wildwood to do battle with the enemies of his Lord.

Thus begins the long tradition of Romance in the Franciscan Movement. And by Romance here is not meant Romantic in the modern sense, but the Romance of the Middle Ages of Saint Francis, who lived from 1182 to 1226. Medieval Romance located the hero's struggle against evil "within the heart and soul of each protagonist. The Education of the hero in the virtues appropriate for both Christian and courtly life lay at the center of the Romance plot. The development of character, requiring self-testing, reflection, and emerging self-knowledge now came into focus."[2]

Not only did Francis act out his life like a Knight and Troubadour of Christ, but like the Troubadours whose songs he knew, he summed up his life in a Swan Song, his "Canticle of the Creatures," an Incarnational poem that praises God through, with, for, in and on behalf of all creatures. Francis sang this poem two years before he died; and though we no longer have the music (if it was ever written down), we do have the words of this first great Italian poem sung in the Umbrian dialect and rendered in English as the final poem of this anthology.

It is Francis himself, then, who sings the first Franciscan poem; and he is followed by others of the early Franciscans, including Jacopone da Todi, who wrote in the generation after Francis and who gave us among other classic poems, the "Stabat Mater," still sung on Good Friday throughout the world. Other friars composed popular spiritual poems and songs for the edification of the Faithful. And in time these Franciscan songs and poems became songs and poems about Saint Francis. A literature of homage began to grow steadily, from Henri d'Avranche's versified "Life of Saint Francis" to the poems contained in this anthology.

In modern times Saint Clare, too, has begun to emerge, not only in connection with Saint Francis, but as a writer and a subject of writings in her own right, she the first Franciscan woman and Foundress of the Second Order, the Poor Clares. Poems of her are here as well, and Saint Francis himself wrote a poetic exhortation for Saint Clare and the other Poor Ladies of San Damiano, as Francis dubbed them:

> Hear, little poor ones, called by the Lord,
> sisters from many places and provinces:
> Live always in truth so you may die
> in obedience. Do not long for life
> outside; that of the spirit is better.
> With love, I pray you, use discreetly
> the alms which the Lord lends you.
> You heavy with sickness and you
> tired of their sickness, all of you,
> bear it in peace. This fatigue you will
> sell for a dear sum, and be crowned
> in heaven with the Virgin Mary.[3]

And Clare herself pens beautiful poetic passages in her Letters to St. Agnes of Prague, who had relinquished royalty to take the hand of Christ as a Poor Clare. The Fourth Letter to Agnes, especially, is, in its images and style, much like a prose poem. The editors have selected this extraordinary letter as the penultimate poem in this anthology.

All of which is to say that the lives and writings of Francis and Clare are the very stuff of poetry. As the poems in this anthology demonstrate, Francis and Clare are icons that call from poets, ancient and new, songs of homage, songs of veneration, songs that try to understand something of the mystery of their love of God and all God's creatures, a mystery hinted at in these beautiful words of Thomas Traherne, the English poet and clergyman who died in 1674:

> You never enjoy the world aright till the sea itself floweth in
> your veins,
> till you are clothed with the heavens and crowned with the
> stars: and
> perceive yourself to be the sole heir of the whole world: and
> more than so,
> because men are in it who are everyone sole heirs, as well as
> you. Till
> you can sing and delight in God, as misers do in gold, and
> kings in
> sceptres, you can never enjoy the world.

—Murray Bodo, O.F.M.
Casa Papa Giovanni
Assisi, Italy

NOTES

[1] Thomas of Celano, Second Life, 165, author's translation from *Through the Year with Francis of Assisi,* Cincinnati: St. Anthony Messenger Press, 1987.

[2] Hester Goodenough Gelber, "Revisiting the Theater of Virtue," *Franciscan Studies* 58 (2000).

[3] Author's translation.

FRODO AS FRIAR: THE SACRAMENTAL IMAGINATION

The great and unsurprising (to admirers of Francis) popularity of the *Lord of the Rings* movie trilogy, and the ongoing success of Tolkien's written work in general, is surely the result, not only of his considerable scholarly and creative talent, but of his notion of the literary imagination as well. As the Englishman spells out so beautifully in his "On Fairy Stories," his idea of the imagination—a vision which, if it doesn't come directly out of Saint Francis, surely expresses the same artistic, sacramental response to the world—finds its root in the belief that what is created in each successful literary case is a living thing borne of a living culture. It can't be parsed or dissected without damage being done. Or, to put it another way, because it is a holistic co-creation (to lift from Peter Maurin) on the part of the teller, be that person the scop of *Beowulf* or a twentieth-century writer of "fantasy literature," the vision which informs it is necessarily seamless to its heart and soul. And this is especially so in a hope-brimmed way when it comes to the Catholic imagination because the good God doesn't need to limit his revelations, using only those things bathed in or having come to evangelical light. He can and often does use the dark humus of the imagination, pagan or Christian. He uses the unconscious, myth, archetypes, the feminine, fertility, history: any and every good thing; and because of that fact, any and every earthly thing on the planet is sacred. ("...This bread, which human hands have made...") After all, Saint Paul in his letters encourages his pagan listeners to read their own poets!

What's nice and revolutionary about Tolkien's work is that he recreates a pre-Judeo-Christian world steeped in a loving God's sacramental presence and abiding concern. Saint Francis had done something similar years before. And he did it with the given world itself. (Tolkien obviously had to have seen as much himself, or else he could not have created his fictional world.) But who, after all, knew and loved that real world better than Francis, who called both the moon and death "Sister"? Who else heard both the flowers and their roots as the very speech of God?

Like no other fallen human being, Francis understood and loved nature. A good medieval, he understood that God spoke through his first book first, yes; but who has ever been able to plumb its mysteries as Francis did! He chose to die naked on the ground before going to his God because he was in love with the planet, too. And who would've been better able to appreciate all the different voices, poets, who speak to him, after him? He wouldn't have fretted over much about the dogma behind these poems, though he knew and accepted all of the church's teachings, including those present-day unspeakables: sin and hell. He would have seen the hand of God working through each fractured earthbound poet, too, as each reaches toward the Perfect. And he would have given God glory for each go.

And I think, surely, he would have embraced Frodo too: a character as humble as Neville Longbottom, a hero who never in his wildest dreams could've ever become one. And so he did! Like Francis, like the priests in *The Power and the Glory* and *Deep River*.

Ah, humility, here is *thy* ring!

—David Craig

A Note on Francis and Clare

It is ironic that so many books, including this one, have been written about Saint Francis, who was extremely leery of books, fearing that they might become personal property and objects of pride, thus diverting their owners from full devotion. But Saint Francis' fierce purity and the absoluteness of his conviction compelled witnesses, and so he has been chronicled in story, song and image since his death in 1226. Saint Clare, too, has been the subject of thousands of paintings, stories, poems and biographies, and the lives of these two Assisi saints are so intertwined it is hard to separate their stories.

Francis was born in 1181 or 1182—the date is not certain— to Pietro di Bernardone and his wife, Pica. His father was a well-off cloth merchant who often took his young son on buying trips. The young Francis was a lighthearted gallant who often used his father's money to impress his friends. As many boys of his time did, he seemed to think of himself as a romance hero, until brief war experience showed otherwise. And even as a young man his lightheartedness was mingled with spells of piety.

One day when praying at the cross in San Damiano he received the instruction to rebuild the church. He took the instruction literally, and stole goods and money from his father to rebuild the crumbling edifice. He did not know until later that the instruction was more metaphorical: he was to rebuild the church. The total commitment to Christ that this larger task required made it necessary for him to put his family behind him, which he did during the famous incident in which he publicly removed his garments and gave back all belongings to his father, declaring himself God's henceforth. The bishop wrapped him in his cloak.

Francis was to form the Lesser Brothers and revive the spirit of self-denial and total devotion that seemed to be slipping away from the Church. He lived a life of full renunciation of the world, and was known for his holiness and his legendary love of animals, his embrace of the feared and detested lepers, his preaching and example of peace and brotherhood, and the self-denial he practiced to the point of ill health but did not insist that his followers practice so severely as he himself. He received the pope's approval of his rule. Toward the end of his life, he received the Stigmata while praying at Mount La Verna, thus fulfilling his desire for his life to be fully an imitation of Christ's.

Clare came from the wealthy family of Favorone di Offreduccio, who wanted her to marry well. She was born in 1194 into a life of privilege, but early showed an unusual piety. When she heard Francis preach during her eighteenth year, she was inspired to give up her comfortable life and live "after the manner of the Holy Gospel." She desired to be like Francis and live as a beggar, owning nothing. Clare's family had determined that she should marry well. But she had a mind of her own and wished to live simply and prayerfully, devoting her life to the service of Christ.

Therefore, she ran from her family to Francis, desiring to live like him. On Palm Sunday 1212 Francis clipped off her hair as a symbol of her renunciation; the clipped locks still gleam in the glass case in the reliquary of the Santa Chiara church in Assisi. But Francis thought it would not be safe or seemly for women to live as he did, in the open without shelter, and lodged her temporarily with the Benedictine nuns. With his help, Clare was to start the Poor Ladies, later the Poor Clares, where the women lived lives of renunciation and prayer; this was the Second Order of Saint Francis. Eventually Francis installed Clare and her followers in the San Damiano church, where he had heard God's command. Clare spent the rest of her life at this church, now her convent and refuge, praying and fasting with her sisters.

It is amazing how quickly the Lesser Brothers grew from a handful of devoted followers of Francis to thousands, and how the Poor Clares, too, took root and became an institution of devotion and meditation lasting through the present day. By the time Clare died, there were 150 communities of Poor Clare sisters throughout Europe.

Francis visited the Poor Ladies seldom after they were established but always remained a subject for their deep veneration. Although he himself and the Lesser Brothers had nothing, he always made sure the nuns were provided for. When Francis died, exhausted and used up, in 1226, his body was brought to the convent so that Clare could say good-bye to him. She continued to lead the sisters until her own death in 1253.

The bodies of the two saints remain in their churches in Assisi; eight centuries later, their spirits continue to inspire not only Catholics but many others.

—Janet McCann

DIRECTIONS FOR PILGRIMS

As you enter Assisi, beware;
danger lurks on Mount Subasio.
Vipers coil where
laurel and ginestra grow.

You're an intruder from a time
imagined, not here where beer
bottle nudges jonquil and Saint
Francis lives in souvenirs.

But be consoled. Your Francis
your Clare, still dwell here in
those who hobble and hunger,
who draw from wounds a hymn.

—MURRAY BODO, O.F.M.

FROM *THE DIVINE COMEDY*

Many critics believe that the cord Dante refers to in the very middle of hell, the cord which summons up the Geryon he and Vergil will ride down to the lowest level, that of fraud, is a Franciscan one: evidence perhaps that Dante may have belonged to the Franciscans or had been one in his youth. Either way, the level of esteem accorded to Francis here is high indeed. (The translation is Henry Wadsworth Longfellow's.)

In the second fragment, which comes from *Paradiso*, Canto XI, Saint Thomas Aquinas, a lesser-known Dominican at the time, sings the praises of Saint Francis. (In the next canto, XII, Bonaventure will sing of Dominic.)

FROM CANTO XVI OF THE *INFERNO*

I had a cord around about me girt,
    And therewithal I whilom had designed
    To take the panther with the painted skin.

After I this had all from me unloosed,
    As my Conductor had commanded me,
    I reached it to him, gathered up and coiled,

Whereat he turned himself to the right side,
    And at a little distance from the verge,
    He cast it down into that deep abyss.

"It must needs be some novelty respond,"
    I said within myself, "to the new signal
    The Master with his eye is following so."

Ah me! How very cautious men should be
    With those who not alone behold the act,
    But with their wisdom look into the thoughts!

He said to me: "Soon there will upward come
    What I await; and what they thought is dreaming
    Must soon reveal itself unto thy sight."

Aye to that truth which has the face of falsehood,
    A man should close his lips as far as may be,
    Because without his fault it causes shame;

But here I cannot; and, Reader, by the notes
    Of this my Comedy to thee I swear,
    So may they not be void of lasting favour,

Athwart that dense and darksome atmosphere
    I saw a figure swimming upward come,
    Marvelous unto every steadfast heart,

Even as he returns who goeth down
    Sometimes to clear an anchor, which has grapped
    Reef, or aught else that in the sea is hidden,

Who upward stretches, and draws in his feet.

—DANTE ALIGHIERI

FROM CANTO XI OF THE *PARADISO*

The one was all seraphical in ardour;
    The other by his wisdom on earth
    A splendour was of light cerubical.

One will I speak of, for of both is spoken
    In praising one, whichever may be taken,
    Because unto one end their labours were.

Between Tupino and the stream that falls
    Down from the hill elect of blessed Ubald,
    A fertile slope of lofty mountain hangs,

From which Perugia feels the cold and heat
    Through Porta Sole, and behind it weep
    Gualdo and Nocera their grievous yoke.

From out that slope, there where it breaketh most
    Its steepness, rose upon the world a sun
    As this one does sometimes from out the Ganges;

Therefore let him who speaketh of that place,
    Say not Ascesi, for he would say little,
    But Orient, if he properly would speak.

He was not yet far distant from his rising
    Before he had begun to make the earth
    Some comfort from his mighty virtue feel.

For he in youth his father's wrath incurred
    For certain Dame, to whom, as unto death,
    The gate of pleasure no one doth unlock;

And was before his spiritual court
    Et Coram patre unto her united;
    Then day by day more fervently he loved her.

She, reft of her first husband, scorned, obscure,
    One thousand and one hundred years and more,
    Waited without a suitor till he came.

Naught it availed to hear, that with Amyclas
    Found her unmoved at sounding of his voice
    He who struck terror into all the world;

Naught it availed being constant and undaunted,
    So that, when Mary still remained below,
    She mounted up with Christ upon the cross!

But that too darkly I may not proceed,
    Francis and Poverty for these two lovers
    Take thou henceforth in my speech diffuse.

Their concord and their joyous semblances,
    The love, the wonder, and the sweet regard,
    They made to be the cause of holy thoughts;

So much so that the venerable Bernard
    First bared his feet, and after so great peace
    Ran, and, in running, thought himself too slow.

O wealth unknown! O veritable good!
    Giles bares his feet, and bares his feet Sylvester
    Behind the bridegroom, so doth please the bride!

Than goes his way that father and that master,
    He and his Lady and that family
    Which now was girding on the humble cord;

Now cowardice of heart weighed down his brow
    At being son of Peter Bernardone,
    Not for appearing marvelously scorned;

But regally his hard determination
    To Innocent he opened, and from him
    Received the primal seal upon his Order.

After the people mendicant increased
    Behind this man, whose admirable life
    Better in glory of the heavens were sung,

Incoronated with a second crown
    Was through Honorius by the Eternal Spirit
    The holy purpose of this Archmandrite.

And when he had, through thirst of martyrdom,
    In the proud presence of the Sultan preached
    Christ and the others who came after him,

And, finding for conversion too unripe
    The folk, and not to tarry there in vain,
    Returned to fruit of the Italic grass,

On the rude rock 'twixt Tober and the Arno
    From Christ did he receive the final seal,
    Which during two whole years his members bore.

When He, who chose him unto so much good,
    Was pleased to draw him up to the reward
    That he had merited by being lowly,

Unto his friars, as to the rightful heirs,
    His most dear Lady did he recommend,
    And bade that they should love her faithfully;

And from her bosom the illustrious soul
    Wished to depart, returning to its realm,
    And for its body wished no other bier.

—DANTE ALIGHIERI

THE ANNUNCIATION OF FRANCIS

I did not come to him on bended knee
clutching a stalk of lilies and a message from God,
dressed in a gown effulgent as fire.

I came out of the darkness of earth
from the place where the poor creatures wait—
the claws that walk upon the pebbled ocean floor

the four legged with their strong haunches
and tremulous upright ears
long tongues unrolled in devotion or fear

the winged things who wanted their own sermon
ringdoves and waterfowl
even the vultures who put aside their carcass

to sit in a circle and feed on his preaching
silent as a gathering of saints.
The loops that circled their necks,

shackles laid across the canticle
on their bones, were rent loose by his words
till they too settled nearby like souls.

When he appeared to the brothers of the order
as he darkened in death, I was there,
signifier of the five wounds.

It was my luminous hand that held the glass
to catch the thick venetian red
dribbling like wine from his side.

—JAN LEE ANDE

HOW CLARE, CONVERTED FROM THE WORLD BY FRANCIS' INFLUENCE, ENTERED THE RELIGIOUS LIFE (A.D. 1212)

Thirsting to flee the world, the maid addresses her teacher and asks when or how it could be done. Her teacher, fearing to delay further what the Holy Spirit had breathed into that virgin vessel's midst, lest she, the mirror that true Wisdom had cleansed for Himself be fouled by the world's dust, exhorts her to go out to receive the palms on the coming Palm Sunday, finely dressed, and then on the next night to exchange her world's joys for the tearful way of the cross, abandoning the doomed company of this life. The maid carries out her spiritual father's bidding and enters the church, and Clare shines bright in the ladies' company. When all the congregation hastened to receive the palm branches, Clare held back her step, overcome as it were by modesty; and by divine nudge the bishop goes down to her and offers her the palm. There are certain foreshadowings here: the bishop had a sense of one whom Christ had already inwardly betrothed to himself. And as her teacher instructed, Clare hastens to the Holy Virgin's chapel on the following night, leaving her father's house: The Friars receive her with many lights, happy about the rich prize rescued from the snares of the world; and immediately after her hair was cut she takes leave of her accoutrements and retinue, migrates from the world, rejects Babylon's dung and all illicit delights, and renounces everything that's sordid. What she had earlier conceived about her marriage to Christ she now gives birth to outwardly; in the Virgin's holy chapel she pledges herself to the Son in a bond of firm love, bestowing the signs of her virginal flower to Christ. Happy betrothal, happy profession, chaste embrace, pleasant love, sweet bonding, diligent effort, fervent love! Great is her faith, wonderful her honoring of God, through which her devout mind was wedded to God, fragile flesh to the divine Word, the lowest to the highest and the vile to the precious! Her wise teacher arranged that the girl be brought to St. Paul's, until the heavenly Bridegroom would dispose what he wanted to happen next.

—ANONYMOUS (TRANSLATED BY DANIEL J. NODES)

THE ROOMS OF ST. CLARE

> One has only to go into any room
> in any street for the whole of that
> extremely complex force of
> femininity to fly in one's face.
> —Virginia Woolf

Hers is the mystery of rooms.
The room from whose window she watches
Francis walk across the Piazza San Rufino
and into whose tapestried forest
      she withdraws
to seek the unicorn's white horn
that brings her to that other room
where Bishop Guido places
the palm into her open soul.

Rooms open on rooms.
St. Mary of the Angels, the room of vows
that open onto the nuns at Bastia,
the monastery on Mount Subasio, and
San Damiano with its rooms God has prepared for her,
each room conforming to the contours of her soul
like a fitted wedding dress.
There at San Damiano

she crosses the threshold
            into the Royal Chamber.
Above the marble altar-bed she sees
herself in the mirror that spoke to Francis.
She's radiant, calm, pure with desire.
She kneels and the room
opens upon mansions of possibility;
other brides cross the threshold with her,
fill the rooms of their own espousals.
Rooms spill out into streets of their village,
a courtyard around whose well they gather
to draw water, talk their own domesticity.
They gather for church
            like women inside Assisi's
walls. They sing psalms, share the Bread of Life,
after which they pass
            a further threshold
into Lady Poverty's dining room where Clare
blesses another bread
            crossed with want and penance.

But it is the steep ascent from choir
through the narrow passageway
            opening
into their Bridal Chamber
that lifts Clare and the Poor Ladies above routine.
For there is the room of redemptive suffering where
Clare ministers to her sick sisters,
lies bedridden sewing albs and altar linens.
There she opens the door, kneels
before her Eucharistic Lord, and
prays away the threatening advances
of the Emperor's mercenary soldiers.

There in the room of consummations
she holds her Rule that holds
all the rooms of the Poor Ladies' lives.
She presses the Book of Rooms to her heart and
Crosses the final threshold into all the rooms
of her life
       now graced with Him
who is the mirror she enters without effort,
without shattering the glass that
holds her image inside His.

—MURRAY BODO, O.F.M.

THE LETTERS OF CLARE TO AGNES OF PRAGUE

And Clare takes up her pen.
    She dips it in black
        indelible liquid.

She draws the letters that form the words
    that name the way
        into the Bridal Chamber,

to the place of waiting
    for the soundless step
        that arrives without walking,

without opening or closing doors
    without movement
        except the movement of her heart,

the Bride, hearing no sound
   yet knowing he's there
      beyond the hearing.

He—the paradox—in whose embrace is union and virginity, in whose touch is chastity sealed. The words flow from the pen, her hand moving where her heart leads—farther into the room where He adorns her breast with precious stones, pierces her ears with gems shimmering like blossoms in springtime. His left arm circles her waist, his right circles her head with a crown, golden for holiness. It is the Crucified Christ who steals thus into her bedroom, with whom she merges as with her own image in the mirror that is the crucifix, the corpus like the mirror's bronze disk convex with desire.

Can she write what she sees?
It is herself she sees in Him
   whose embrace, though rough and poor
      as the unbleached wool she wears,

is as familiar as her own arms
   wrapped round her shivering body
      standing in the dormitory's frigid morning.

She writes:
   Gaze into that mirror each day
      until you see your own face within it.

That contemplation wherein Jesus' face
   becomes your own,
      adorns your whole body

with the flowers and garments
   that are all the virtues:
      At the border of the mirror

the swaddling clothes of poverty;
    at the surface, the laborer's tunic of humility;
        in the depth of the mirror

the nakedness of Love
    hanging from the wood of the cross,
        Love Who's become the mirror of those

who long to mount the cross with Him,
    who cry out,
        Draw me after You

embrace me happily,
    kiss me
        with the happiest kiss of Your mouth.

—MURRAY BODO, O.F.M.

ST. CLARE DIES AT HER MIRROR,

August 11, 1253

I've lived in the labyrinth, love its scrubbed walls,
doors whose thresholds lead to the brass basin, worn
where a Sister's foot soaks warm in my laving hand.
Portals here billow into linen albs, their shadows
arching into gates through which Saracen horses pound
toward their own retreat; the blinding ciborium whirls
warriors, spins our lacing bobbins. Winter roofbeams
groan their vows beneath God's weight, His rough beard
scratches the eaves like a storm of olive branches.

I've embraced the labyrinth, the basin's womb become
a mirror for seeing around corners; looked into, it's

the crucifix that spoke to Francis, Christ's wounded,
bent face now a lucid window onto my own riddle
recumbent on the stone pillow. On the roof God hops,
sparks in a gossip of sparrows. Small, brown, winged,
my soul flits through death's dark mirror, into light.

—MURRAY BODO, O.F.M.

ST. CLARE—SUMMER NIGHT, SCATTERED CLOUDS

> *"Brother Leo, what do you think I saw*
> *reflected on the water down in that well?"*
> *"My Father Francis," said Brother Leo,*
> *"You would have seen the moon that was shining*
> *in the sky."*
> *"No, Brother Leo, I saw there the face of our Sister Clare."*
> —The Little Flowers of St. Clare

A crescent moon plays with clouds
above St. Clare's Basilica.
It slips behind the waves and
reappears, unnoticed where
bright floodlights hold her docked tomb
still beneath the lolling clouds.
I almost hear water drip
from the skiff-like moon floating
above the mother ship's prow.

—MURRAY BODO, O.F.M.

ST. FRANCIS OF ASSISI

How strange it must have seemed to see him
Strip off his clothes in front of his father
And his bishop and stand naked before
The two of them, proclaiming his trim
Love for Lady Poverty in the dim
Light of a medieval moon whose core
Was shaken by this would-be troubadour
And the song he sang that made wealth seem grim.

How strange he must have looked, buck-naked,
Hugging a tree, like another Adam
Rediscovering earthly paradise,
His love of nature forever encoded
Among the rocks and rivers, in the dam
Of the beavers, in downy nest of mice.

—JOHN BOWERS

A SARCOPHAGUS AND THE SINNERS

We came to you from afar,
Because we want to be good,
O sarcophagus.

We seldom manage.
Perhaps never.

Evil torments us
Like black goats.

We torture the people
We love.

We wrong our neighbor
Whom we want to help.

Behind our every sacrifice
Stands egoism
Like a skinny prompter.

One beautiful poem
Is more important to us
Than a good deed.

That's why we speak to you
By way of crying,
O sarcophagus.

A long examination of conscience
Can only be told in tears.

Sail on the brackish water of our tears
Saint Francis.

Sail on a crusade
Against our sins,
O, singing Middle Ages.

Sail, sail,
You bird song.

Can a new man be born
From a tear?

Create us from our tears,
Create us from our cries,
From our stormy cries,
Dear Saint Francis.

Your sarcophagus reposes
On our prayers
As on expectant columns.

—ROMAN BRANDSTAETTER (TRANSLATED BY
KAZIMIERZ AND JUSTYNA BRAUN)

GIOTTO'S "ST. FRANCIS PREACHING TO THE BIRDS"

They've arrived at his bare feet as calmly as the poor
who have come to expect the flayed habit from his back.
They attend in pairs—the way it was once said souls first
were made—indifferent to the one tree standing for all
knowledge here on earth, and from which they cannot eat.

Magpie, goose, and crow; sparrows in their impoverished
suits; heron, rooster, and descending doves, have shaken
loose of skyways and cloistered bush to feed in the aura
and flat blaze of evening. But his extended hand offers
a blank perspective, and so they consider the intangible

kingdom of prayer, seeing that bread will not fall
to them all their days, that finally this burnished glow
might be every reward, all there will ever be beyond
the invisible example, the finite comfort of his words—
"Brethren, lesser cherubim, true apostles to the trees,

so that you shall be spared a degree of faithlessness
in this world, I reveal to you these wounds, the drab
roses and candle ends of my arms, the last things I have
to celebrate the explicit ecstasy of air...feast then
on this sparsely flavored dust, and doing so, be restored

to the bright dominion of wind. Go as our good reminder
above the confabulating leaves, the glorious and simple
sign of your wings admonishing the weight of our desires—
sing there the spirit unadorned, spellbound as smoke
rising into these gold and uncompromising fields of light."

—CHRISTOPHER BUCKLEY

THE LEPER'S RETURN

—a gift of Saint Francis

He had grown used to the fear he carried
to the hearts of all he passed along the road.
And the chagrin he bore inside became

a bitterness far worse than the fetid taste
that never left his mouth. He could not bear
to stay near town for long, nor could he ever

walk far enough away. His days were marked
in varied degrees of suffering, varied
degrees of shame. So when he saw the young man,

trembling, stand awaiting him in the road ahead,
the leper felt the weight of his long burden briefly
lift, and when the young man rushed to embrace him,

the leper startled to the fact of his own body
gently held, and held in firm, benevolent
esteem, and when he felt the kiss across

his ruined cheek, he found forgotten light
returning to his eyes, and looked to meet

the brother light approaching from the young man's

beaming face. Each man blessed the other
with this light that then became the way
that each might travel every road thereafter.

—SCOTT CAIRNS

FRANCIS MEETS A LEPER

He heard the bell toll, erratic
in a palsied hand, and smelled
the goatish scent before he saw
the figure moving in mist on the road
to Assisi, a traveler gloved and shod,
as was the law, to hide the sores,
a man's inhumanity, missing fingers
and toes, and tried to unmask the face,
slack muscles showing nothing
but astonishment, lower lids keeping
eyes open always to our providential decay,
flesh soft and thick as rotten wood.
Francis saw in bleary eyes, near to him
as his mother's as she loved him,
a brother, then someone dearer, wrapped
as he'd seen others in his father's cloth
that first had profited English shepherds
and the weavers of Ghent, a skin
bleached white as bone, a flower blazing
in snow, so close to perfection it could
only decay. Francis did the only thing
he could, sun rising high enough now
to burn away the mist. He unwrapped

the face, studying lineaments fashioned
by a master's hand, image and likeness
of the death that beautifies all living.
He closed his eyes and kissed.

—DAVID CITINO

THE TWENTY-ONE FRANCISCAN MARTYRS: NEW MEXICO, 10 AUGUST 1680

i.
High coyote yelp at moonset
And owl-murmur—
Dawn of San Lorenzo's Day:

Fray Juan Bautista Pío
Broke the night's fast with goat's milk
And left the *convento* in Santa Fe.

His turn at Holy Mass in Tesuque.

At the last steep turn
He reined the pied mule
Hard right at the puddled wall,

Where a brazen lizard
Glared back his glance;
Hay, hermano diablo, he said and laughed.

The pueblo wholly unpeopled,
Blank with mid-morning sun,
The friar followed a dog's bark

Into the near ravine,
A dry, shrubby *rñto*-bed
Churning with silence.

One of the baptized women screamed.

Then it was a short lance.
Iron-tipped for bear or elk,
Snapped under his chin,

And cinched his jaws,
Lifted his weathered tonsure,
But failed to break it.

His lay companion
Scurried the news to Santa Fe,
That day of dread—San Lorenzo's Day.

ii.
Given the spare chronicles, such a re-creation,
Based on what few details we think we know,
Carries no disrespect, may in fact show
A certain praiseworthy identification
With martyrdom that benefits the soul—
A pious fiction with truth as its goal.

iii.
This little we do know, names and places:

> At Galisteo, two, Fathers Juan Bernal and Domingo de Vera;
> At windy Pecos on plains-edge, Fernando de Velasco (30 yrs
> a missioner);
> In Nambé, Tomás de Torres, of Tepozotlán;
> At San Ildefonso, two, Luis de Morales and Brother Antonio
> Sánches de Pro—"who from the Descalces passed to the
> Observancia";
> In Picurís, Padre Matías Rendón;

Two more in high Taos, Antonio de Mora and Brother
    Juan de la Pedosa;
On the Turquoise Trail at San Marcos, Fray Manuel Tinoco;
In Santo Domingo, three, Padres Francisco Antonio de
    Lorenzana, Juan de Talabán (*custodio habitual*), and Joseph
    de Montesdoca;
At Jemez, Padre Juan de Jesús, far from Granada;
On Acoma, near the sun, Lucas Maldonado (*definidor actual*);
At Alona, the Castilian, Fray Juan de Bal.

As the sun moved west,

At lost Xongopavi, Padre Joseph de Truxillo, of storied
    virtues;
In Aguatubi, Fray Joseph de Figueroa;
At old Oraibi, Joseph de Espeleta (30 yrs a missioner)
    and Agustín de Santa María.

Where possible and with sufficient warning,
They no doubt consumed the Host,
Thus sparing assassins a greater sin.

iv.
Another day will come,
At once vacuous and rabid,
When the charge-card shall reign.

Reconquered Santa Fe
Is dispossessed again.

Franciscan zeal for souls,
Baptism and sweet oil of chrism:
"Tools of rank imperialism!"

New Age pimps the kivas—
Discounted kachinas.

It is late in the day.

v.
If you're like me, "a pilgrim sore bereft,"
Follow the Paseo de Peralta
(Though old Don Pedro was no friend of friars)
And climb the steep little hill to the left.

The most reliable guidebooks agree
That the view from the Cross of the Martyrs
At sunset repays a tourist's efforts,
But what you seek is more than you will see.

Recite the names and places, try to pray
Like the child you were and still hope to be.
Do not presume to warrant martyrdom,
But prime yourself for San Lorenzo's Day.

—WILLIAM BEDFORD CLARK

WHY I COULD NEVER BE A BUDDHIST

> *"All that exists is the movement of the breathing."*
> —Shunryu Suzuki

I wake up early and lie uncovered
on the summer bed
staring at the white closet doors,
listening to the hum of the fan
which has drawn in the cooler night air—
your ghost-form next to me
wrapped tightly in a sheet.
I would love to be as empty

as the rice bowls of the dead,
but the squirrel on the hickory tree outside
with a nut in his mouth,
reminds me of the need to save,
and the mirror on the wall
containing a small oval edition of this room
is a medieval warning against vanity.

I hear the faint hum of a plane
and picture a woman in the window seat
crossing her legs and opening a magazine,

then I think of the Wright Brothers,
who never married,
working in their bicycle shop,
spoked wheels hanging from nails in the walls.

Even the sight of my own feet,
crossed on the bed,
reminds me of the sinewy feet of the saints
that I used to kneel before as a boy—
the feet of St. Bartholomew,
the feet of St. Anthony of the Desert,
braided with muscle,
the feet of St. Sebastian pierced with arrows,
and the benevolent feet of St. Francis,
who in one painting
is leaning back in rapture
outside the mouth of a cave
while behind him an iconographic rabbit
peeps out of a stone wall,
a little symbol of God knows what.

—BILLY COLLINS

ASSISI

Even in February the buses came and climbed the hill,
The Umbrian light an angel's wing in cloud,

Glowing from some unknowable source in an Italian painting.
No wonder some gave a life's savings to see Saint Francis's

City of pink stone. No wonder we couldn't help loving
Those arching crypts, blue and storied as a child's heaven.

What we want to remember, we do. How he could keep on giving
His one robe, unashamed by love. How his love never failed

The sick, the poor, the criminal. Even a war in Arezzo
Simply disappeared, like rain into sunlight, Saint Francis

Undoing the daily harm no one could ever alter in his life.
The demons said to be in all of us laid down their weapons,

Taken by such tenderness. Everyone was forgiven in Giotto's
    picture.
Saint Francis went on, unable to sleep, so many blessings

Still needed to be given. He walked all the way to Mt. La Verna.
When we close our eyes, we can see him hold out his hands.

The wounds bleed into them and into his body, the marks
Of another life. From then on, he grew thinner until he was

Gone, his love absolute. At least once, some one saw him
Come back, robed in light. Giotto would have us believe

It was only a dream of what we cannot stop imagining.
We came back all winter; listening to the monks tell his story

Until word for word, we could repeat it.

—ROBERT CORDING

ON THE DAY FRANCIS DIED

The Wolf of Gubbio howled until Sister Moon
Centered herself in the star-tilted sky,
And then he wolfed the darkness down
Until Brother Sun curved over the watery rim of earth.

The birds who gathered in the square
Said that Francis gave the Guinness book sermon then
And blessed them with the brokenness of bones,
Remembered now like fresh baked bread.

The Brothers brought him naked, wrapped in linen
Like a philodendron leaf about to unfold,
To Claire to reach out toward beyond the grate,
As prayer had reached and would the world to grasp.

It was an ordinary day, other than that a saint had died.
Yet so it was the Wolf of Gubbio
Brought a songbird fallen from its nest into that square,
Reached up and, by his weight of grief, rang out the bells.

—CHET COREY

FROM "THE LEGEND OF THE THREE COMPANIONS OF SAINT FRANCIS"

Chapter I
His birth, vanity, frivolity and prodigality, how he became
generous and charitable to the poor.

Dignity underfoot, he turned his life
into a gabbling goose of a performance, a wonking
high wire poetic act, him singing so loudly

from stumps, imaginary instruments,
in horrible French, that everyone who passed
just had to watch—him dare himself,
paint himself into one spiritual corner after another,
until he had no options but severest Truth,
in the boisterous rhymes of the troubadours,
set right, by a grin so local it owns the world.

It was his wide-eyed father who'd taken the first stride:
naming his son after a country—
where they knew their fabric,
where they valued life's buckled and measured step
as well as its print.
         But his French mother,
she prayed for the very breath of God: Giovanni!
No. No! His father wanted him here,
among a carafe of friends, ridiculous neighbors.

And so Francis learned to trade the prayer
the best cloth was for the smiles of new friends.
After work, his pals would ring in the chorus
his money made: a cascade of coins, grace,
surrounded as they all were,
by the cold stones of the only night.

It was all Francis could give them.

(Was he vain,
or just so caught up in his enthusiasms
that they'd begun to make their own demands?)

He'd sew rags to more expensive stuffs,
embracing, again, that widow, want,
knowing he could not, needing to tell everyone
that as well. So he became a jongleur,

a determined clown, standing in the breech
between the sorrowful truth of this world
and the fleeting faces of his friends.

So courteous in manner, speech,
even beyond his exaggerated, broadly beaming
self-conscious parody—everyone knew
he could name his own future.
He loved to pose, but only because it promised
what was, in some way, already here.

One day, though, cut off by a customer's
quick exit, he saw the constructed moment collapse,
the fiction in how he was living.

But what of those things beyond his making?
What about the squalor, the ugly, the poor;
what about those with nothing to give but their need?
It was the wound again, what they all felt,
the abyss which could not be filled, nor avoided,
the one that preceded and followed,
made an island of his laughter.

Given all this,
where could he live?

Chapter II
How he was imprisoned during Assisi's battle with Perugia and
of the two visions he later had, wanting to become a knight.

He camped for his new peers,
as if he were that troubadour Bernart de Ventadorn,
fresh from the castle's bread kilns—
for the laughs he knew: dancing, skirt lifted
on cold stones, singing too loudly to birds

out the small window, telling rhymes
of fearful Assisian Knights.

Why *should* he worry? The world was new enough;
every morning everywhere mists came,
only to be burnt away by the sun,
so many new people around by afternoon,
no one could've guessed.

And so when the weight of the hours
began to take the measure of one knight's need,
Francis would not back down.
He flanked the man, feinted, sang in bad langue d'oc
because he was a merchant's son:
"What do you think will become of me?
Rest assured, I will be worshiped
throughout the whole world."

Eventually released, he let the past go,
everything except his need to test himself,
until a dream chided him—
for his too-modest goals!
There he walked though *his* castles:
legions of rubied, runic arms, surpassing
even his carefully chosen own. And shields!
Walled fields of them, bronzing sunlight.

Chivalry so moved in him the next morning
that he gave all his clatter away.
Friends laughed, wondered if his stirruped feet
were (ever) on the ground. But Francis, for his part,
he figured, yes, yes, he could give them this;
he could show them the answer that was possible
before its time, be its fool, its peacock.

When asked the reason for his glow, Francis
answered largely, as if he were one:
"I shall become a great prince."
Why else were dreams given, but to make us princes
(and holy fools) before we would become one
(preparing him to turn the world upside down)?

He got as far as Spoleto: "Who can do more for you?
The lord or the servant?...Go back."
And just as the dream had given him a chest to fill,
this voice took his every measure.
What would be asked of him, he wondered?
How could he be a princely knight and wear
the holy ribbons of church too? And what of his lady-
who-must-be-in-waiting?

The next morning came, and Francis,
sitting on a stump, rejoiced,
kept these marvelous engines, his future,
as best he could,
stabled in his junket-heart.

Chapter III
How the Lord visited Francis's heart for the first time filling it
with marvelous tenderness that gave him strength to begin to
progress spiritually in looking down on himself and all vanities,
in prayer, almsgiving, and poverty.

A party for the new money, and more,
from the very stems of delight: ladies—
each of his pals, now enjoying what was left
of the tipsy night, some steps in front of him,
their misplaced lives, as ever, just out of reach.

Francis, ever the jester, chose to walk behind,
scepter in his hand, dressed as he was,
in silks and tatters, knowing by now that rags
really were riches, either way: metaphor for the chase,
the shell game of wealth and fame;
for that, or for the more quiet, obvious need.

But how could he get his friends
to know what was real, and missing:
what demanded so much?

Then, noticing, as if for the first time, what he gripped—
his scepter—he understood!
Yes. Yes. He was just the fool for this job!
And surely this was no place for half measures!

They came back to him, their captain in mirth
elsewhere, looking up, seemingly lost
in the glorious conflagration of stars.
Pausing, they wondered aloud:
was he getting teary-eyed
over the girl in the crimson stomacher?
"Yes, you are right," he answered.
"And I shall take a wife—more noble, wealthy,
and beautiful than any you have never seen."
But they didn't laugh when he said, "Poverty...
the one we all chase without knowing it...."

And after that day, he never denied an alms
to anyone who asked
in God's only name.
Heaping his absent father's table with begged bread,
Francis piled his want high,
like the joyful exasperation it had become—

in front of his mother, grieving: that the world
would, so soon, begin hammering away
at his white-hot enthusiasms,
would bend him—all out of shape.

But Francis had no future
to wait on. He walked to Rome,
pressed his face between the bars,
tossing his last flightless bird,
bag of coins, high and crashing down
onto Peter's tomb.

Once outside, he roused a beggar,
swapped clothes. He needed to try on his life.
Yes! Yes! These would help him keep himself in a line,
would help him keep the world far away,
with its trumpets, bandied names.
This way he'd never confuse himself again!
He'd wake up, sitting next to new brothers: lepers,
dew on his rags.
          He sang loudly,
played fiddlesticks on the open road,
so that the world would be forced to mark him,
hold him to what mattered.

Once back, he didn't share his secret,
because he was betrothed to a lady, Poverty,
a woman hidden in so much beauty
that a look from anyone at all
would have violated, surely, their first
intimate steps.

—DAVID CRAIG

FRANCIS (FROM KAZANTZAKIS)

How funny, sharp nosed gentle monk;
walking and dreaming of revelation,
joyful with thoughts of your forest retreat.

But here in Rome you're a beggar still,
prisoner in thin damp streets,
company to skulking stray curs,
witness to daybreak garbage orgies.

"Step back, holy man, back in dark doorways."

Beyond hospitals, deeper than coffins,
the Roman she-wolf, Remus and Romulus
wait their masters crying out
for sanctity on the Spanish Steps.

And now my friends sit,
bleeding like doctors,
fingers pressed upon their ears,
reading stories of slaves and saints,
of leather and brass, and curses in stone,
of masters, of enemies, of screams in the Tiber.

Did you hear, Senora Bernardone,
that strange wailing from out in the hills?
It happened on Sunday when you were at church;
It came and now the rain has turned warm,
your shutters are locked, the kitchen empty,
your husband the victor: red face, square shoulders,
is saved from sin by a pair of stone lions.

Now we search in the vineyards for Francis,
we search although he has never lost *us*,

but watched us dancing among the shadows;
cement shadows of ox-carts and airplanes.

Forgetful, drunken
we turn in our madness,
hypnotized, we dance tarantellas.

—CARLO DANESE

NIAGARA FALLS

> "Brother Leo, to be a saint means to renounce not everything
> entirely, but also everything divine."
> —Saint Francis of Assisi

*   *   *   *

Last year we lived in Torre Gentile
        a small village a short ride from Assisi.
I had to find out more about
        the only name I had ever chosen.
What moved me in Assisi was Cimabue's St. Francis
        not the saintly one in Giotto's frescoes
looking too holy and wise to touch,
        a religious superman lifting buildings,
casting out demons.
        Cimabue's Francis would get his ass kicked
in the gym class locker room. Frail, homely, big ears.
        They might call him that—Big Ears, Dumbo.
But he wouldn't be fun to tease—too quiet.
        He wouldn't get mad. Maybe he'd even flunk gym
for refusing to box. The kind of kid
        you wouldn't mind having sit across

from you in home room. He'd give a kind of comfort
      you'd be embarrassed by. *But he's a nice kid,*
you'd say, almost apologetically
      when someone called him a sissy.

*   *   *   *

Cimabue and de Zurbaran.
I have held postcards of those paintings,
one in each hand. They don't look
anything like each other
except for the robe.
One haunted, one at peace.

If the kid sitting across from you in homeroom
gets beat up in gym class every day
for a week or two, what happens to his spirit?

I am haunted and at peace.

Niagara Falls.
Step by step, inch by inch
I'll take all that free water falling anytime.
All that free romance, anytime.
Sister Water… precious and pure.

Why do we want to go over
in a barrel? Why do we want
to go up in the tower?

Moe, Larry, Curly, come on out here
you crazy stooges. Let's give them
a big hand, our hands slapping together
our mouths gaping open.

I want to be saved, I am going over,
I can't help myself.

*

We are almost home, driving
in the chill of this autumn evening,
the sky so gray that darkness
will be a relief, headlights
will be a relief. My wife
is sleeping softly against my shoulder
exhausted by bread
and the long numb hours
of our broken radio.
I hear a siren, but she does not stir.
I make the sign of the cross—
something I'd never let her see me do,
a superstition, old habit.

It is how I was taught, and though I know
it won't do a bit of good
for whoever's in the back
of that ambulance, I want to at least
signal the air, signal my four corners
and this darkening world:
we are human and we're going to die.

I say to the person lying prone
zooming past: I am sorry
and I hope it's not now.

I say to the dead raccoon
by the side of the road:
we're in this together
though I know you don't believe me.

It is true that
no living man can flee

Sister Bodily Death.
But I am singing this song
to keep her away.

But I too will tire, and sleep.

*

We are carp swimming up river, Mama,
all of us, even you. I hold the steering wheel
in one hand. The other rests
on my wife's knee. My wallet against my ass
tells me little about who I am.
It is the prayer book this world insists on.

The sound of the tires hisses in my ears
like rushing water.

If I was a saint, I might
scoop out my dashboard full of change
and toss it to the wind.
But I am counting it out
to pay my toll.

—JIM DANIELS

SAINT FRANCIS AND THE SEVEN VISIONS OF THE CROSS

O truly poor Francis, patriarch of our times,
Yours is a new banner, emblazoned with seven crosses.
Much has been written on the meaning of each,
But I'll spare the reader and try to be brief.

The first vision, soon after your conversion,
Was one of a noble palace. Within, it was filled
With shields marked with the cross—
The shields of those entrusted to you.

Another time, as you prayerfully meditated
(The mere remembrance of the vision
Always reduced you to tears), you caught fire
in the love of the crucified Christ.

That Christ you saw said to you,
"Come and lovingly embrace this noble cross;
If you would follow Me, become as nothing,
Hate yourself and love your neighbor."

Still later, when again you were meditating on the cross,
In clear, strong tones He called you thrice by name
And then, "My Church has lost its way—
Set it once more on the right path."

On the fourth occasion, Brother Silvester
Saw a golden cross shining over you,
And your blazing words put to rout
The cursed serpent that had encircled Assisi.

In similar fashion, as Brother Pacifico gazed at you, Francis,
Worthy of all praise, he saw a cross of two swords—
One reached from your head to your feet,

The other followed the line of your outstretched arms.

As Saint Anthony was preaching, Blessed Brother Monaldo
Saw a vision of you in the air, on a cross,
In the act of blessing your friars; and then,
According to the account, you vanished from sight.

The seventh apparition came as you prayed with great devotion
On the craggy heights of La Verna—
An awesome vision of a six-winged seraphim, crucified.
It sealed you with the stigmata—side, hands, and feet.

The man who hears a brief account finds this hard to believe,
Yet many there were who saw these marks
While you were still alive and well,
And on your death many came to touch them.

Among others, Saint Clare came,
Bringing with her her sisters;
Greedy for such treasure she tried in vain
To pull out those nails with her teeth:

The nails were made of flesh, hardened like iron,
The flesh was as fair as a child's.
It had lost the traces of the many winters;
Love had made it radiant, beautiful to gaze on.

The wound in your side was like a scarlet rose.
All that saw wept at the marvel:
Its likeness to that of Christ
Made the heart sink into an abyss of love.

O happy weeping, full of wonder—
Joyful weeping, full of consolation!
How many tears of love were shed there,
To see and touch the new Christ's wounds!

They flowed freely as the friars gazed upon this vision
Of fiery love. The precious balsam of holiness
That lies hidden in the heart
Had burst forth from the wounds of Francis.

That towering palm tree you climbed, Francis—
It was with the sacrifice of Christ Crucified that it bore fruit.
You were so closely bound to Him in love you never faltered,
And the marks on your body attested to that union.

This is the mission of love, to make two one;
It united Francis with the suffering Christ.
It was Christ in his heart that taught him the way,
And that love shone forth in his robe streaked with color.

The burning love of Christ, whose depths are lost to sight,
Enfolded Francis, softened his heart like wax,
And there pressed its seal, leaving the marks
Of the One to whom he was united.

I have no words for this dark mystery;
How can I understand or explain
The superabundance of riches,
The disproportionate love of a heart on fire?

Who can measure the intensity of that fire?
We only know that the body could not contain it
And it burst out through the five wounds,
That all might see that it dwelt therein.

No saint ever bore such signs upon his body—
Sacred mystery, revealed by God!
It is best to pass over this in silence;
Let only those who have experienced it speak.

Wondrous stigmata, manifestation of the holy,
You give witness to the awesome presence behind the awesome
    sign.
All will be clear at the end, when the last joust is over,
In the presence of those who follow the cross!

O my arid soul, dry of tears, run—take the bait;
Drink of these waters and never turn away
Until you are drunk with love.
Oh, that we might die at this sacred spring!

—JACOPONE DA TODI

ON SAINT FRANCIS AND THE ENEMY'S BATTLES AGAINST HIM

O Francis, beloved of God,
Christ made Himself manifest in you!
The deceitful Enemy, adversary of the Lord,
Dreading that his lost power would devolve to man, approached
him and through fraud led him
To disobedience and to the loss of paradise.
The Enemy glorified in his triumph,
For with man's fall he was raised,
And became the Prince of this World.
Then God became man, wounded him mortally,
And wrested from him that dominion.
The humility of God changed the Enemy's fortunes,
And holy poverty checkmated him.
Long after his defeat the Devil tried again,
And man did not escape his snares.
Seeing the Enemy was carrying the day,

The Lord God sent in the cavalry with an able commander;
Saint Francis was chosen to lead the troops,
And he accepted into his ranks only those
Who despised and rejected the world.
The three great steeds that would carry them into battle
Were poverty, obedience, and chastity.
Francis wore the arms of his Lord,
Who loved him with such a great love
That He marked him with His own signs.
And so intense was the love in Francis's heart
That his body was adorned with five magnificent jewels.
He was like a fig, whose great value is not visible to the eye,
But is hidden in the center, honey-sweet.
The Lord God then showed Francis how to skirmish,
How to deliver blows and how to take them,
And taught his tongue the language of peace.
The sight of Francis struck fear into the Enemy,
For he much resembled the Christ, who with His cross
Had once before stripped him of his prize;
"If he is the Christ, the victory will be His;
Against Him there are no defenses.
O misery, to be defeated by such an enemy!
But I will not lose heart, I will tempt him
Nothing ventured, nothing gained!

"Francis, take care—
that strict fast you've begun will kill you."

    "I fast with discretion,
    For the body, properly disciplined,
    Is a good and useful servant."

"The whole world knows you are a saint;
We have seen in what esteem the Lord holds you,

May His holy name be praised."

> "I want to conceal the good in me,
> And show the world I am a sinner.
> My heart is with the Lord
> When I bow my head low."

"What do you plan to do? Don't you want to work,
And with you earnings help those in need?"

> "I shall go about in rags and beg for my bread;
> In my love of God I go about like a drunken man."

"What good will that do? You will die a miserable death,
And your followers will grieve that you left them penniless."

> "I will stay on the true path, with neither purse nor bag;
> I have told my followers they must never touch money."

"Go then into that lonely wood
With your ragged band of heroes;
In that solitude you will edify man,
And God from His throne will smile on you."

> "I did not come into this world to shirk my duty;
> Pressing one, I will lay siege,
> Pitching my tents around your citadels."

"I fear your tactics: with this Order of yours
You will take many souls away from me.
At least leave me the women—
Your friars shouldn't be mixing with them."

> "I have upsetting news for you:
> I have founded an order of sisters,
> And they too will wage war on you."

"What woman would ever have the impudence
To move against me, the conqueror of the world?"

> "In the valley of Spoleto lives a virgin,
> Of sovereign virtue, a temple consecrated to the Lord,
> Clare, the daughter of Donna Ortolana."

"Married people should not mix with friars and nuns—
You can let them go, leave them under my patronage."

> "I will trouble you even more:
> I have founded an order for married penitents."

"At least leave heresy, your enemy, alone;
If you touch that it will be too great an offense."

> "I mean to fight the heresy that dwells in your mansions,
> And those infected with it I'll have thrown into prison."

"Oh, I am poor and wretched indeed!
What has happened to that sharp hook of mine?
You've put a bit in my mouth and are reining me in!
Francis, you have annihilated me and retaken the world,
So bereaved me that I am utterly destroyed.
Enough! I shall call on the Antichrist,
Whose coming has been prophesied."

> "And I will deal you both the final blow.
> I will win back the world and free those you
>   have imprisoned,
> Sharing with them the striped robe of the fool,
> Mad with the love of the Lord."

"The prophetic texts do not reassure me;
The last part foretells the victory will be yours:
Then truly will I be undone."

In this harsh and bitter struggle
Many will be wounded and slain,
And the rewards of the victor
Will be more than ample.

—JACOPONE DA TODI

THE POOR LADIES OF SAN DAMIANO

Step down, out of the sun, into this crypt:
still life, with candlelight, and bride;

she has waited seven hundred years
for the bridegroom to claim her body;

she lies, in a glass casket, beyond glass walls;
watch, and your own face is watching back. Name her—
clara, bright, translucent—Clare;
and something less, not-life, not-death: dusk.

The face has a talcum pallor,
the fingers have the sheen of candlewax.

Precious, preserved, a dried flower.

*

Purple toadflax clings
to chinks in a high brick wall
in a market town in Ireland;

on glass-spiked wall-tops
lilac and laburnum droop,
their purple grapes,
their tresses of golden hair.

Poor ladies. Behind their walls
they struggle to emulate
the image of the Bridegroom, crucified;

outside, dealers thump with sticks
on the flanks of cattle;
trucks go by, their stench of dung,
the gasps of jostled animals.

*

Clare, like Penelope, sat by her mirror
embroidering an alb for Francis;
when their eyes met he was watching
far beyond, and only distorted shadows

passed on the mirror's surfaces.
Outside, olive trees drooped with a weight of fruit;

the density of flesh, if she could only
shuck it off, allow the blossoming

of love, of ecstasy, untrammelled, pure;
Clare, in quiet, offered up her life to God

bringing a coarse, dark fabric as a dowry.

*

In Ireland, poor ladies behind their grille
have given up their lives for peace;
as wedding blessings they send out prayers,
and rosaries of olive-coloured beads.

Today, above Assisi, mirage fighter jets
burst from the sun to shatter
the convex mirror of the sky.

We come, tourists, wedding guests,
step down out of the sun into the crypt;
whispering, and jostling, we are ushered past;

we know she died, Juniper and Angelo are witnesses;
she stepped through the mirror
into God's image, leaving her flesh
for the curious eyes of centuries.

—JOHN F. DEANE

FRANCIS OF ASSISI 1182 : 1982

Summer has settled in again; ships,
softened to clouds, hang on the horizon;
buttercups, like bubbles, float
on fields of a silver-grey haze;
words recur, such as light, the sea, and God;

the frenzy of crowds jostling towards the sun
contains silence, as eyes
contain blindness; we say—may the Lord
turning his face towards you,
give you peace;

morning and afternoon the cars moved out
onto the beach and clustered, shimmering,
as silver herring do in a raised net;
this is a raucous canticle to the sun.

Altissimu, omnipotente, bon Signore...

To set up flesh
in images of snow and of white roses,

to preach to the sea on silence,
to man on love—
is to strain towards death
as towards a body without flaw;

our poems, too, are gestures of a faith
that words of an undying love
may not be without some substance;

words hovered like larks about his head,
dropped like blood from his ruptured hands.

Tue so'le laude, et onne benedictione…

We play, like children, awed and hesitant
at the ocean's edge;
between dusk and dark the sea
as if it were God's long and reaching fingers
appropriates each footprint from the sand;

I write down words, such as light, the sea, and God,
and a bell rides out across the fields
like a man on a horse with helmet and lance
gesturing foolishly towards night.

Laudato si, Signore,
per sora nostra morte corporale…

—JOHN F. DEANE

FRANCIS, THE SAINT

How often had the Wind taken me in Its beak,
tried smashing me to pieces by dropping
me down on the mountain? But this time there's no stopping

my thoughts from secreting, attempting to break

through the rock and take root, even though this desolate peak
is no place for them, these vultures hopping
about and with one quick snap of the head, slopping
them down. Without much on my mind (so to speak)

I run off, limbs flapping, my thoughts-become-
holes whistling with the provocation of Wind.
Filled with the forgotten, I seal my hands,

feet, and side with some drippings from the Sun.
I've been thinking—thoughts I cannot begin
to teach animals. Never mind humans.

—MARK DECARTERET

MANIC MONSTER

Cardinal on my forsythia, rot:
may your less than kumquat-sized hot heart
freeze like a snow-embalmed cherry.

Bug-eater, high on natural speed,
hiphopping while singing of love,
yo! Spring's mindless, repetitious rap,

syncopating feather ball, must stop—
Strange white things are dangerous.
Its eyes are the sleek ends of BB gun barrels,

its mouth is a cat's out of luck.
How have I become this monster?
Hitler on bad days, says some bird-brained expert,

sometimes approaching God as a poet,
must take pills. Stupid tweeter,
I suppose he's right…Sweet, nervous bird,

I'm sorry, I'm sorry—Come back!
Tomorrow I'll talk like St. Francis again
while *Frate Uccello* eats worms.

—THOMAS DORSETT

THE PRINCE

He must have heard them rustling
in the twilight around Florence.
Many years before, Francis
heard them praising God;
what did faith prove?
Believers are ventriloquists;
life is not some dummy's dummy;
he knew trees better:
more brutal than Borgia
yet with consciences
cleaner than Christ's,
each leaf is the Prince's
original tongue…
Florence needed it;
how could he translate
nature's politics into a book?
Perhaps by taking a good look
at what I'm seeing now:
children playing;

innocent as trees, they battle
over toys in a small circle
where grass has been annihilated
by a maple's shade.
One laughs, the other cries…
Precursor of Darwin,
he knew life was a struggle
and that the fittest wins.
An honest view, a practical book.
Still trees, I'm not convinced;
reading between leaves,
I believe even yet—
St. Francis will have the last word.

—THOMAS DORSETT

UNDER WATER

Saint Francis submerged,
I preach to indifferent fish.
As sun and darting sides meet,
light forms silver columns;

minnows and one wholly drowned
shepherding his flock in silence—
Seems like a mad forum.
The venue of my Bubble Sermon

pass, prose swimmer, if you must—
Entropy the music of
bald rocks encircled by algae—
All you see is the poet's tonsure.

Not even God can make *you* trust
his golden wrecks, exposed to tides,
broken down yet satisfied
with something to say like the sea.

—THOMAS DORSETT

SAINT CLARE

*She refused to marry when she was twelve and was so impressed by a
Lenten sermon of Saint Francis in 1212 that she ran away from her
home in Assisi, received her habit, and took the vow of absolute
poverty. Since Francis did not yet have a convent for women, he
placed her in the Benedictine convent near Bastia, where she was
joined by her younger sister, Agnes. Her father sent twelve armed men
to bring Agnes back, but Clare's prayers rendered her so heavy they
were unable to budge her.*
—John H. Delaney, *Pocket Dictionary of Saints*

1. THE CALL

First I heard the voice throbbing across the river.
I saw the white phosphorescence of his robe.
As he stepped from the boat, as he walked
there spread from each footfall a black ripple,
from each widening ring a wave,
from the waves a sea that covered the moon.
So I was seized in total night
and I abandoned myself in his garment
like a fish in a net. The slip knots
tightened on me and I rolled
until the sudden cry hauled me out.

Then this new element, a furnace of mirrors,
in which I watch myself burn.
The scales of my old body melt away like coins,
for I was rich, once, and my father
had already chosen my husband.

2. BEFORE
I kept my silver rings in a box of porphyrite.
I ate salt on bread. I could sew.
I could mend the petals of a rose.
My nipples were pink, my sister's brown.
In the fall we filled our wide skirts with walnuts
for our mother to crack with a wooden hammer.
She put the whorled meats into our mouths,
closed our lips with her finger
and said to Hush. So we slept
and woke to find our bodies arching into bloom.
It happened to me first,
the stain on the linen, the ceremonial
seal which was Eve's fault.
In the church at Assisi I prayed. I listened
to Brother Francis and I took his vow.
The embroidered decorations at my bodice
turned real, turned to butterflies and were dispersed.
The girdle of green silk, the gift from my father
slithered from me like a vine,
so I was something else that grew from air,
and I was light, the skeins of hair
that my mother had divided with a comb of ivory
were cut from my head and parceled to the nesting birds.

3. MY LIFE AS A SAINT

I still have the nest, now empty,
woven of my hair, of the hollow grass,
and silken tassels at the ends of seeds.
From the window where I prayed,
I saw the house wrens gather
dark filaments from air
in the shuttles of their beaks.
Then the cup was made fast
to the body of the tree,
bound with the silver excrescence of the spider,
and the eggs, four in number,
ale gold and trembling,
curved in a thimble of down.

The hinged beak sprang open, tongue erect,
screaming to be fed
before the rest of the hatchling emerged.
I did not eat. I smashed my bread to crumbs upon the sill
for the parents were weary as God is weary.
We have the least mercy on the one
who created us,
who introduced us to this hunger.

The smallest mouth starved and the mother
swept it out like rubbish with her wing.
I found it that dawn, after lauds,
already melting into the heat of the flagstone,
a transparent teaspoon of flesh,
the tiny beak shut, the eyes still sealed
within a membrane of the clearest blue.
I buried the chick in a box of leaves.
The rest grew fat and clamorous.

I put my hand through the thorns one night and felt the bowl,
the small brown begging bowl,
waiting to be filled.

By morning, the strands of the nest disappear
into each other, shaping
an emptiness within me that I make lovely
as the immature birds make the air
by defining the tunnels and the spirals
of the new sustenance. And then,
no longer hindered by the violence of their need,
they take to other trees, fling themselves
deep into the world.

4. AGNES
When you entered the church as Bastia
holding the scepter of the almond's
white branch, and when you struck
the bedrock floor, how was I to know
the prayer would be answered?
I heard the drum of hooves long in the distance,
and I held my forehead to the stone of the altar.
I asked for nothing. It is almost
impossible to ask for nothing.
I have spent my whole life trying.

I know you felt it, when his love spilled.
That ponderous light. From then on you endured
happiness, the barge you pulled
as I pull mine. This
is called density of purpose.
As you learned, you must shed everything else
in order to bear it.

That is why, toward the end of your life,
when at last there was nothing I could not relinquish,
I allowed you to spring forward without me.
Sister, I unchained myself. For I was always
the heaviest passenger,
the stone wagon of example,
the freight you dragged all the way to heaven,
and how were you to release yourself
from me, then, poor mad horse,
except by reaching the gate?

—LOUISE ERDRICH

TRANSUBSTANTIATION

[St. Francis and St. Clare]

> *Love does not exist in and of itself*
> *As a substance: it is the accident of substance.*
> —Dante

1

In the ciborium, the body.

2

Friars carry torches. Flames and shadows
of flames swim along the chapel walls.

3

Light spills onto them at the altar where she bows
her head, stares into the planks of the floor. She offers
her hair forward, offers because she wants
him to touch her, even if only her
scalp, even if only, his blade.

4

He lifts his hand, tenses his arm in hesitation.

5

The light trembles, turns and shrinks from the torch fires to the
ciborium and then
bends into the bowl of holy water. Her
strands ignite and glow
as white flames, burning autumn stalks.

6

He lowers his blade into her brightness, lifts the strands
and begins to cut. The threads of her hair fall and recoil still
glowing.

7

Beyond the altar, they are one
flat shadow, ashes of the body, an offering
to God.

—MARCENE GANDOLFO

AT THE EXHUMED BODY OF SANTA CHIARA, ASSISI

So here you are, queen of the chiaroscuro, black girl,
backstitching on us. What would you mend coming back up
intact? Is it so crooked a thing
you want us

to see? Here we are, the temporary ones
at your deathsill. The sky over our irreversible progress
impure and sometimes glad
is blue. The sky over whether I leave him

or not, over myth, extermination camps, and Bruna's hands
making lace faster than I
can see, is blue. Blue over your body in its afterlife
on its back in its black dress with gold trim

looking out on us the unused.
As if the flesh were the eternal portion after all,
here it is, your blunt modesty, pure,
even after a ton of dirt, six hundred years,

and the emblem in the human mind
you have become. As if this were always
what flesh is a declension of: more flesh. Beneath motion
more flesh,

beneath daylight and rot and law....Can it be true?
the night wind softening and softening the olive trees till
what I see of them is where they were
just then,

calling that *olive trees*. I touch
that love. That deep delay. So and so you loved,
so and so you left before the age of twenty-one calling it
faith, founding an order of

such nuns, all dressed in black, black veil over
the face. In order not to hide from us, that veil. In order
to be seen.
     I lean upon your nowhere now.

—JORIE GRAHAM

SAINT FRANCIS AND THE BIRDS

When Francis preached love to the birds,
They listened, fluttered, throttled up
Into the blue like a flock of words

Released for fun from his holy lips.
Then wheeled back, whirred about his head,
Pirouetted on brothers' capes,

Danced on the wing, for sheer joy played
And sang, like images took flight.
Which was the best poem Francis made,

His argument true, his tone light.

—SEAMUS HEANEY

THE MIRACLE OF THE NAILS

One day in mid-September when Saint Francis
was approaching 43, he received the Stigmata.
A hole in his side oozed blood. He needed
special socks to cover the wounds the nails
had made and kept on making in his feet,
because these nails were actually nails,
not just the prints of them, they were
hooks of iron under his soles. His hands
with the nails in them were torn and bandaged
and tucked up his sleeves so he only showed
the fingers. This went on until the day he died,
and Francis sang because he was happy
and safe in the knowledge that he would gain
Heaven, which Pope Gregory said he did,
so then Francis was a saint. I rode
my bicycle around town today thinking
about this. I kept my bare feet free
of the sprocket and I sang my song
to the humming of the tires. And I came home
to continue singing as if to the blue sky
where the roof left off and it was all blue
above the windows and the trees. As I bent
in blessing on my neighbors and my kinsmen,
I practically bled all over the neighborhood.

—MICHAEL HEFFERNAN

SOLVITE TEMPLUM HOC

For the dedication of the Portiuncula,
Franciscan University of Steubenville,
23 October 1987

Your parable struck lightning in the eyes
Of him whose Papal audience you sought,
For deep beneath the billows of his thought
A half-remembered dream began to rise.
The Lateran basilica he viewed,
The Temple of the New Jerusalem
Whose patrons (moneylenders, all of them)
Have set it tottering and made it crude.
But then a dirty beggar takes control,
And in a trice restores his Father's house.
A Samson in reverse, the beggar bows,
And, hands upon the pillars, holds it whole.
His Holiness now sees the dream fulfilled:
He sees in you the church you will rebuild.

—JOHN R. HOLMES

SORA VERMA

1 Celano 80, 2 Celano 165, Job 17:14

Among the fibers of your tunic's thread
Your Sister Worm and Brother Flea squirm in.
You bless them as they penetrate your skin
And leave it irritated, raw, and red.
But even then you bless the shiny bites
Of insects as your body's glow of love

For God, who in his majesty above
Created here below all living mites.
For He who gave your tiny brothers breath
Is source of every life, both great and small.
To cherish life, you must preserve it all,
Until you give it back to God in death.
Give thanks to God for plagues of pests like Job's
And all the teeming life beneath your robes.

—JOHN R. HOLMES

II

LEO, BROTHER LITTLE LAMB OF GOD, TO
LADY CHASTITY

Now, my friends, far to the south
and inland is a mount
that smokes from its streams at morning.
All upon that mountain grow the trees,
and in the shadow of the trees
blooms one blood-red rhododendron.
     None has seen it. None touched.

Under the blood-red rhododendron
in the witching of the million trees,
a milk snake loops his magic circle.
No color is lacking from his scale
by slanted light. Think of his
against our Lady's glory, scale
against hair that, blowing in silence,

sets the first of day aflame.

I woke and saw a girl swell
in the bark of trees. I saw summer
turn womanly down into the valley
with high breasts and a thousand arms of flowers.
I reached to touch;
    flesh undid the dream.

The village wife come to fill her pain
sends her hair behind as rain
sends musks of forests.
I do not know whether this requires of me
homage or judgment. Christ forgive;
I stand and drink as one drinks
thunder from the sea.

To what love shall I sing?
I have nothing but love, love abundant,
love unspent, untarnished, rising wave-like
till the sea is drowned.
Who would love me like this back again?
Love is all I keep, the word unsaid,
the hand withdrawn that the heart might seize.

Once our master watched me watching.
He said, "Leo, come in and say
what a woman's walk has told you.
If it is wrong, we are too small to know."
So I spoke of a Lady who is love,
who for my fidelities
    is lost to me forever.

My Lady Wanting, without you is no lover.
Without you is but talking and the need again.
If a woman cut her hair in quiet,

let the strands blow across the grass
for the moles, the nests of birds,
I'd love her then for what she could not give.
        Lutenists have touched their throats

for music in a woman's praise until
I have no taste for any further sweetness.
But for another savor,
bitter and beautiful.
If she fell darkened of her eyes,
bereft of all the silver stirring,
        shadow then in shadow, black

but for her break in black space,
I would love, as love is empty.
I would as the gardener loves
the singing west that is the rain,
as the soldier loves the enemy who
bleeds beside him on the lost field.
I would love, Queen Chasteness, as a man

loves what fades by morning from his clenched hand.
Day comes to light the space in my heart.
She enters then, this Lady,
careful that I look away.
I wait; who's loved in emptiness
is loved forever.
        Lady, rain your hair around me.

—DAVID BRENDAN HOPES

DUNS SCOTUS'S OXFORD

Towery city and branchy between towers;
 Cuckoo-echoing, bee swarmèd, lark-charmèd, rook-
  racked, river-rounded,
The dapple-eared lily below thee; that country and town
 did
 Once encounter in, here coped and poisèd powers;

Thou hast a base and brickish skirt there, sours
 That neighbor-nature thy grey beauty is grounded
Best in, graceless growth, thou hast confounded
 Rural rural-keeping folks, flocks, and flowers.

Yet ah! this air I gather and I release
 He lived on; these weeds and waters, these wells
  are what
He haunted who of all men sways my spirit to peace.

A reality the rarest veinèd unraveller; a not
 Rivalled insight be rival Italy or Greece;
Who fired Thomas for Mary without spot.

— GERARD MANLEY HOPKINS

FIRE AND ST. FRANCIS

1.
As he sat eating by the fire one night
a spark was lifted on a wisp of air
and set on the folds of cloth that wrapped his groin.
But when he felt the heat so near his flesh
he wouldn't raise his hands against the fire
or let his worried friends extinguish it.

You mustn't harm the flames or spoil their play,
he said to them. *Don't these bright creatures have*
as much a right as I to be happy?
For seconds his disciples stared as the flames
climbed up the cloth and nearer to his skin.
And he, without a qualm, turned to his bowl.
At last their knowledge of the world prevailed.
As one, they leapt on him and held him down,
smothering the fire with dirt and what was left
of the soup that had been their evening meal.
When he returned, embarrassed, to his prayers,
his genitals swung through holes scorched in the cloth.

2.
Laid on the fire, the iron throbbed red with heat,
and then turned orange beneath the doctor's breath.
The saint's face twisted in a burst of pain,
and the doctor marked it with a dab of soot
so he would know where to apply the iron.
To calm himself, the saint spoke to the flame:
Brother Fire, be gentle on my quenching skin
that I might have the love to suffer you.
Composed, he signed the cross above the fire,
which bowed its many heads in seeming grace
beneath the blessing motion of his hand.

3.
He held the ember in his hand, and braced.
But soon the burning grew too great to bear,
and Francis set it gently back into the fire
and wept. His hand was oozing from the burn.
A new disciple asked him why he wept

since when you hold an ember in your hand
you know what to expect. Francis wrapped the hand
in a grimy strip of cloth torn from his robe
and said, *When I was young I had a dog*
that snapped my hand whenever I touched him,
and every time he did I held it out again.
About the hundredth time, he licked my wrist.
Perhaps he just grew tired of biting me,
or maybe with my pain I'd earned his trust.
About this fire, however, I don't know.
I dream some day the flames will flit
around my fingers like a yellow bird,
a tulip leaping on my fingertips.
But so far it won't take me for a friend.

—ANDREW HUDGINS

THE LADY CLARA SEES SAINT FRANCIS NAKED

I. *Porziuncula*
After Vespers, the Lady Clara flies
down narrow monastery stairs into October
night, a woman summoned. Her sisters heard
no messenger. No rapping had breached
San Damiano's silence, yet the Lady runs.
To see her slog through stinking marsh
might appall those accustomed to nuns enclosed,
but Clara and her Poor Ladies need no grille
to still the world. No stone could wall in
or out the fire, the piquance of their prayer,

nor bind her and God any closer than they are now,
running together.
    That light dancing through the trees?
Fireflies? No, nor swinging lamps—but the clear,
hot light of this woman's determination, burning
away whatever dares hinder her. She has often
thought of the faces of love. If those of spouses
grew more alike in time, then by now she surely bears
Francesco's likeness as much as God's, in whose
image she is made, just as he is clearly imprinted
with Christ as a coin. That is how she knows
it is at this sundown that Francesco will leave her:
because *he* knows.
    Their eyes have not met
since he left the hovel beside her monastery where,
in his last illness, he'd lain for weeks in pain,
fighting mice for the single straw mat. Just eleven years
her senior, now 43, he's nearly broken by his taming
of Brother Ass—what he named his long-suffering body—
finally paying the price: he is dying, and part of her
with him. Tonight. She lengthens her stride.

Umbria's green hills have drained to black
against that burning sky, and rabbits stop, ears
twitching, to catch the music of her passing. Then,
in ruby light, St. Mary's church, *la porziuncula*,
his "little piece" of heaven, shimmers like smouldering
coal. Its pale walls were long ago restored
by his own hands in the early days when he supposed
the brothers' mission was to carry stones,
rather than be them. She assumes the men
have lighted a fire to keep him warm, but
what she took for smoke in circling curls

above the church are birds in billows spiraling
high into wisps, an exultation of larks. Then,
beyond the olive groves, the pitiful sound
of men weeping. Laments lick her face and cling
like shadows. At the door, the friars part,
left and right, as the Lady Clara enters.

Torches cast murky light on stone walls;
it pools on the earthen floor where lies a heap
of rags so small it could not hide a child.
Too late. Strong Leo's arm is under hers.
She pulls away. "Uncover him," she says.
The wet eyes of Leo and Elias—one shy,
one shocked—stare at her. No one moves.
The Lady herself bends to draw the rags away.
"Francesco!"

II. San Rufino
Chiara Offreducio di Favarone was 13
when first she saw him naked. *Piazzo San Rufino*,
paved in round black stones, a froth of ebony
often studded with white and strutting doves,
is echoing with laughter. A festival? Some saint's day?
Only a man steaming by, Pietro Bernardone,
His son in tow, Francesco. Before the church door,
Pietro calls for Bishop Guido's justice, recompense
for the boy's squandering of business assets. Clara
cannot hear his son's reply, but sees the youth
tear free and knows that something is about to break.

The son rips open his tunic as if it were his heart.
Above his head it billows, the finest silk
in graceful sweep. Even at this distance she

recognizes the goods that she and Mother
lately admired at Bernadone's shop, recalls
its softness, like a baby's skin, and wonders
that it could clad a man, even as its airy,
butter-yellow shimmers, settles, a golden buckle
upon Pietro's shoe.

        Francesco's eyes fix upon
his father's. Calmly he sheds layer and layer
of satin brocade and linen until, every tie
severed, he stands calm and naked, no one's mark
upon his skin but God's.

        Noble women turn away
until only simple girls and brazen still gawk.
Young Clara has little thought of men
as anything more than boys gone big. Not shy,
she studies Francesco's breadth of shoulder,
the curve of buttocks, dark threads of hair
at the small of his back, the muscle of his calves.
Until the bishop veils him with his own robe,
Clara stares at the wonder she would never see again:
a naked boy at Christ's door, naked
as Christ himself, and even more beautiful.
The bishop's mantle falls like the silk cover
that hides the golden monstrance after it has held
and beamed that Body which blesses us
just in letting us see it and sends us shaking
to our knees.

III. San Damiano
The second time she did not really see him,
but scullery gossip said that somewhere
in the wintered hills, the strange Francesco

was seen in a child's game rolling heavy snow
into balls, larger and larger, until he'd shaped
six figures he then named and embraced
as his own wife and children. The Lady Clara
smiles, sees in her mind's eye Francesco's hair,
black wet string, his steaming body rolling
in snow like a child. How like him to want it all:
to be his body and escape it, to have sons
and daughters and spouse to expunge his mad
celibacy, to mourn his barrenness, and all the while
laughing at God's fool, himself, knowing
his family would soon melt away.

Behind the kitchen wall, the Lady Clara gulps
cold air like tonic, sucks through her teeth
the dawn, blue as the veins in her mother's wrists.
These memories would keep her feet firm
upon the ground of flesh and blood through the years
when Francesco—in his rare visits—would bare
his soul. Had she not seen that small, swarthy
body as it is, his holiness might seduce her
to believe an angel sat there storytelling. But
who could love an angel? Francesco let go
of bits of cloth as easily as he let go of money
and all else: not in piety, surely not in disdain,
but like one of the birds of the air which, Jesus said,
cared nothing for what they wore, or ate, or drank,
being holy only in being birds.
      When she was just 19,
Chiara too would slip away from father, meet
the brothers here, in this very chapel, and in the dusk
of Palm Sunday, fall into Francesco's hands
that held the shears that cut her off without a penny.

From that day, she'd cling like a cat to what she called
"the privilege of poverty," battling uncles and popes
for the right to have nothing, to depend on no one
but God. Like her name, the Lady was clear
as a flawless mirror polished to reflect the same poor,
naked Christ Francesco had espoused.
                    Just two years
after her own death, the Lady Clara, mirroring Francesco
again, would be enrolled with the saints. A witness
at her canonization testified she'd heard
the Lady Clara remembering: *Once, she said,*

in a vision, it seemed to me I brought to Francis
a bowl of hot water and a towel for drying his hands.
I was climbing a very high stairway, yet quickly,
as if on level ground. When I reached him,
Francesco bared his breast and said,
'Come, and take, and drink.' I did. And when
I'd sucked, he told me drink again, and what
I tasted was so sweet there is nothing
to compare it to. And Francesco's nipple,
from which this sweet milk had flowed,
came away in my mouth, and then, in my hands,
turned all golden, so clear and bright it reflected
all things—everything like a mirror.

IV. Porziuncula
Il poverello—little poor one—is lying on the ground,
skin so dark he's indistinct from earth. Clara
takes him in like the rush of a last breath, notes it all:
the leathery hands, brow so tanned that months
of illness could not pale it; sparse beard greyer

than when she saw him last, ribs like standing ridges
in sand or driven snow, feet dark with dust
that never really washed from pilgrim feet.
His sex lies small and plain and brings no blush
to Clara's face. She who once held him
in little-girl eyes until he disappeared
beneath the bishop's cloak, holds him so again,
no ruddy boy bursting with zeal, but wizened,
used up, serene in surrender again to the only Father
he ever acknowledged from the day she first saw him.
Her eyes shine, full as the moon is of the sun.

From the day in the bishop's courtyard, Francesco
had the habit of giving his clothes away
to anyone poorer than himself, driving
to distraction his superiors who had to clothe him
again. On this October night nothing has changed.
"Let me die naked upon the ground," the brothers
earnestly quote him, as to explain how they would allow
their father to go this way, as if she didn't know
Francesco. The only way he would permit
even these rags to be thrown over him was if
Brother Elias had ordered—"under holy obedience!"—
a last surrender.
　　　His lips are parted, as if he died
singing. The Lady Clara draws her mantel over him.

—FATHER LARRY JANOWSKI, O.F.M.

TESTIMONY OF A ROASTED CHICKEN

Standing in drizzle in the twilit piazza,
Beside the lean Franciscan with his P.A. system,
One of the hilltown's aging bachelors,
Rumpled and plump and damp and pompadoured,
Tells the buzzing mike, the falling rain
And darkness, about Jesus, *la via, la verità, la vita.*
From lit-up bars, a few of us look out at him,
Knowing and pitying and finally indifferent.

How different, later in the bakery,
—Saturday night, buying Sunday's bread—
When he, the sad sack who lives with his mother,
Comes to pick up the meal cooked for him.
Smiling, *la fornaia* brings it out,
A capon fat as he is, trussed and steaming,
And casting over all an enchantment of rosemary,
Making every mouth a well of taste.
"Che profumo, eh!" says the baker, and she grins,
As he whose testimony we ignored
Takes his delectable supper from her hands
And steers it past our eyes into the night
To feast on by himself or with his mother,
While we, watching him go, wish we could have some.

—MARK JARMAN

SAINT FRANCIS IN THE CITY

Speeding by rail through radiant woods
each day on my way to work,
I held Francis' words before me,
mesmerized by his broad vision

of God's world—in love with
Creator and creature alike—
yet jolted by the powerful
claims of this love unfettered,
like fire hydrants let loose
by boys in hot summer streets.

The orange book cover burned
in my hands, as the saint seemed to sing
in humble extravagance:
When you know at last that you have nothing,
no thing, then all you have is gift.

Dispatched east from my suburban Eden
to serve in the city, I discovered with Francis
the ragtag battered beauty of a neighborhood
woven with divine care, where webs of kin
stretched for blocks, then decades, and forever.
For Francis, I found, all creatures are bothers and sisters;
in Southwest Philadelphia all people are aunts and cousins.

At the community center stood an arts studio
where Sister Helen unleashed deep floods of dark beauty
from the hands of old women and small children,
until rainbows rose from heart's canvas
and captive birds flew free.

In her studio appeared her vision of Francis in autumn-orange
brushstrokes, his gaze and hand taming the wolf, still.
On front stoops, old neighbors nodded greetings
as I marveled at their garden boxes,
vestiges of southern life before the great exodus north
from wolf and Jim Crow. Under watchful eye, no bird
or beast disturbed these seedbeds rising from cracked cement.

And somehow, the poverty of God and the stark beauty of it all
took hold and shook the root of my life.
Praise songs rose higher here than the crackle of gunfire
and the rumble rumble of trolleys down the avenue.

At the close of the day, as Sister Moon rose to greet
her Brother Sun, I heard for an instant my heart sing in time
with the glad bells of the ice cream man,
the canine choir, and the double dutch chant of children
playing for their lives
playing for their lives.

—ALEXANDER LEVERING KERN

NAKED

the costly bolts of fine-woven jade or slate the tan cloth unfurl-
ing and cut with stone-sharpened shears are not the foothills
not the mountains not the vineyards not the forests the silver
shears not the wandering cursive of that same stream that slakes
the true minores of Umbria the polished coins that fall daily
into your palms are not the clustered sheep on that distant ridge
not the rain that holds a syllable at the fingertip of each mint
leaf the yellow silk sleeve of some noble Maggiore is nothing
beside the hot tired crowd of watching sunflowers the spiked
filaments of a traveling caterpillar the lighted hair of an infant
twitching in her sleep

dear Pietro dearest Guido as you request here is your money

here my finest clothes

—MAURICE KILWEIN-GUEVARA

SAINT FRANCIS AND THE SOW

The bud
stands for all things,
even for those things that don't flower,
for everything flowers, from within, of self-blessing;
though sometimes it is necessary
to reteach a thing its loveliness,
to put a hand on its brow
of the flower
and retell it in words and touch
it is lovely
until it flowers again from within, of self-blessing;
as Saint Francis
put his hand on the creased forehead
of the sow, and told her in words and in touch
blessings of earth on the sow, and the sow
began remembering all down her thick length,
from the earthen snout all the way
through the fodder and slops to the spiritual curl of the tail,
from the hard spininess spiked out from the spine
down through the great broken heart
to the sheer blue milken dreaminess spurting and shuddering
from the fourteen teats into the fourteen mouths sucking and
    blowing beneath them:
the long, perfect loveliness of sow.

—GALWAY KINNELL

AUNT TIL

I was Bob's sister, second oldest of four sisters, and a sister
of another kind: a member of the Order of St. Francis.

A Franciscan.
Why would anyone want to be a nun?

You may as well ask why St. Francis thought the birds of the air
would sing.

To give unfathomable thanks. To praise God with poverty,
chastity, and obedience.

And for the spiritual romance, for joy unearthly.

My nephew Robert thought I could have been a professor
of political science at St. Francis University.

Was I that sharp?
Instead, I was principal of several high schools and at night

listened to Great Books discussions
from roundtable radio at the University of Chicago.

A Franciscan once said, "A monk should own nothing
but his harp." So my life's music went on,

and daily I sang
from its strings, "The Canticle of the Sun"

to Brother Fire, Sister Water, Brother Daisy, Brother Dandelion.
Was I myself Sister of the Sun and Moon?

"Blessed is he who expecteth nothing, for he shall enjoy
everything," St. Francis said. St. Francis would have apologized

to the cat.
In my seventies, still a sister, I retired to Joliet, Illinois,

where my final song spread even throughout my cancer with this
prayer of our beloved founder,

"Praised be God for our Sister, the death of the body."

—ROBERT KIRSCHTEN

AFTER A DREAM OF CLARE AND FRANCIS OF ASSISI

Alone
at the edge of the sea

he sets the stone in place. Always

the last stone
the stone that has fallen

the broken stone for which there is no use.

His shoulders and the hills are a community now,
when he walks

his shadow loses itself in the grass.

Comes to a crossroads and spins till his bones
fall down in a heap.

From wind and sparrow he gets his bearings;

horizons
pass over him like clouds.

A stranger gives him his cloak, from its holes
he patches together a family.

A neighbor brings him his bowl, he knows
the ways of clay.

The sun sends down its light, so much seed
on good field and bad.

The moon floats in his eyes,
he is learning to see in the night.

The earth had taken him in like a rain,

and when he puts out his hands to the fire,
it runs under his skin like water.

This was her gift, she knew the touch of his hands.

Which is the lighter, the heavier,
the earth that gives, the earth that receives?

He has asked to be planted in the poorest of soil,

like a crop she watches his days
flower and season and fall.

This is her betrothed;

hard the bed that will have no roof
whose blankets are leaves that fall like coins on the floor,

whose nights stretch like a moon

that grows full only to empty its pockets for nothing.
Who here is the richer, the poorer,

the bride, the bridegroom?

—STEVE LAUTERMILCH

TRANSPORT

After the tourist's two blue insomniac nights,
patrols of all that had been lost, botched, or sweet
but severed, during the Albinoni he went off,
up, away, so that if, say, the sudden recall
of his late mother in grainy portrait in her yearbook,
over the captions: "brightest," and—in the quaint patois
of the gentry during their Depression—"most attractive,"
and the despair she may have felt as children and alcohol
supervened: if any such feckless maundering
occurred to him.... Well, off, up and away went she
as well, borne heavenward on the andante's strains.
Two trumpets. One great organ. Peace might well lie at hand.
Peace was at hand. During Martini's toccata in C,

a vision of his tall naked wife, under a tall naked sun,
produced in him in the church a subtle stirring, even
a mild tumescence, which he would otherwise have described
as out of order, were it not that this newer order arched
so beyond any scheme he'd normally posit that within it all
        things
were possible, as they are, it is said, with God, Who
during the Manfredini revealed Himself to our tourist
in what he construed as His human form, His prison garb
stained and rent, His savaged body hefted by men
and women—their countenances looking more angry than
        mournful—
from a loud place like that bar on the corner of Thakurova
and Evropska, which he had walked by that evening on his way
to transport: the Metro, which carried him into this old quarter

in a car along with the beauteous amorous young Czech couple
with their red-tipped white staffs and whited eyes,

then spilled him out to rumpsteak with garlic, alone, and then
to the 9 p.m. concert, alone. During the *Ave Maria*
of Schubert, he saw a joy he hadn't seen in the tears
of St. Peter as rendered faceforth by an artist, Swiss of all
    things,
unknown to him till that forenoon in the Castle gallery.
The wailing weanling calves of his childhood now placidly
    grazed.
The famous small songbirds lit on the outstretched arms of
    Francis.
Peter's tears had appeared only woeful this morning. The hour
    of music
concluded, the tourist walked, though it felt still like soaring,
his cobblestone-wearied heels devoid of any pain,
back into this world, broken and joyous and praying,

"Never to be the same." Never perhaps again.

Church of St. Francis, Prague, July 2003

—SYDNEY LEA

BROTHER IVY

Between road and sidewalk, the broadleafed ivy,
unloved, dusty, littered, sanctuary of rats,
gets on with its life. New leaves shine gaily
among dogged older ones
that have lost their polish.
It does not require appreciation. The foliage
conceals a brown tangle of stems
thick as a mangrove swamp; the roots
are spread tenaciously. Unwatered

throughout the long droughts, it simply
grips the dry ground by the scruff of the neck.

I am not its steward.
If we are siblings, and I
my brother's keeper therefore,
the relation is reciprocal. The ivy
meets its obligation by pure
undoubtable being.

—DENISE LEVERTOV

THE LITTLE BIRDS OF ST. FRANCIS

The little birds fly to ask me what I have seen
in the heavens: I saw your little souls longing.
—Tadeusz Miciński

Our feeble wings
Knock against
A blue windowpane, Lord.
Crowding the trees,
We wait, we sing
Every day at your door.

We gaze at the sun,
Above the trees flutter
And sing since the dawn.
Are we forever
To linger on earth
In this world of yours, Lord?

There is no penance,
Is there no reward?

Lost in our own song,
One day of the year
Among the trees, we'll expire,
Entangled in the leaves.

The wind will lift us,
The earth will receive us
Burying the dry wings.
Will none of us, Lord
Sing in the heavens
Facing your throne?

Is not our singing,
Pleasing to you. Lord?
Our singing choose,
Our waiting use.
From the unknown,
Deliver the birds on high, Lord.

From the ends of the earth
Unbounded and vast,
From pine and beech
From our home
We'll fly, we'll flutter
To your side, Lord.

Whatever your will—
Too deep for the birds—
On earth and in heaven
Your eyes to please,
Your smile to see,
We wing, crowding the trees.

—JERZY LIEBERT
    (TRANSLATED BY KAZIMIERZ AND JUSTYNA BRAUN)

SAINT FRANCIS OF SAN FRANCISCO

But the surf is white, down the long strange coast
With breasts that shake with sighs,
And the ocean of all oceans
Holds salt from weary eyes.

Saint Francis comes to his city at night
And stands in the brilliant electric light
And his swans that prophesy night and day
Would soothe his heart that wastes away:
The giant swans of California
That nest on the Golden Gate
And beat through the clouds serenely
And on Saint Francis wait.

But Saint Francis shades his face in his cowl
And stands in the street like a lost gray owl,
He thinks of *gold...gold.*
He sees on far redwoods
Dewfall and dawning:
Deep in Yosemite
Shadows and shrines:
He heads from far valleys
Prayers by young Christians,
He sees their due penance
So cruel, so cold;
He sees them made holy,
White-souled like young aspens
With whimsies and fancies untold:—
The opposite of gold.
And the mighty mountain swans of California
Whose eggs are like mosque domes of Ind,
Cry with curious notes

that their eggs are good for boats
To toss upon the foam and the wind.
He beholds on far rivers
The venturesome lovers
Sailing for the sea
All night
In swanshells white.
He sees them far on the ocean prevailing
In a year and a month and a day of sailing
Leaving the whales and their whoop unfailing
On through the lightning, ice, and confusion
North of the North Pole,
South of the South Pole,
And west of the west of the west,
To the shore of Heartache's Cure,
The opposite of gold,
On and one like Columbus
With faith and eggshell sure.

—VACHEL LINDSAY

ASSISI AND BACK

It's the train from London to Assisi,
a sort of pilgrimage:
in the diner a dark girl
is staring: I feel my age.

It's the train back from Assisi, and the same
dark girl, suddenly aware:
so she smiles, sits close, intensely
close, and deplores her stare.

I'd like to say, You're lovely, but
as I'm old enough to be
your daddy, a man
must keep some dignity.

But on the platform at the end I give her,
unexpectedly, a kiss.
Her friends shriek, and she
wanders off in, apparently, bliss.

It's pleasant enough
to remember her now,
I seem young and naïve—
she showing me how.

But why was I afraid of her?
Is it cowardice? And this
convergence? Surely not
a hint from St. Francis—

knowing so much more now
than under his vow,
joined properly with poor Clare
up there?

—HERBERT LOMAS

SAINT FRANCIS: STYLE & FAITH

The Holy Ghost is an eloquent Author...
　—John Donne

Some live their faith in style; for others style *is* faith.
Early in the 21st Century, the Franciscan Monastery
Wears a plain robe of clean snow in Washington, D.C.
Where politics talks of peace, religious wars, the wounded.

The street people sleep in the steam on government grates
While the sun melts the night's ice. Someone breaks the ice
To let horses drink near a stable in South Carolina. Friars
Sweep paths penitents will walk on Good Friday, following

The Way of the Cross. The Friars sweep, St. Francis weeps
In the Friars' dreams, in their vespers, in the cloister of Poor
Clares. Franciscans clean the crypts, keep candles burning
For sacred bones, poor souls of the Holy Land, and Shrines.

St. Francis sees the legendary bees, half-frozen, seeking
Food in the Shenandoah winter, the bears sleeping.
The hunted wolf—who seeks St. Francis' sympathy
In Montana—would lick his five wounds. A holy jester

Joined him to wear rough wool, tied at the waist with knots
Of rope, beast-colored. He was schooled by troubadours,
But he begged for stones to heal chapels in disrepair,
Sweeping them clean, he would sleep with the beggars.

Francis loved to sing, even when beaten and bound
As a madman, teased by towns' people, banished
To a cave for flinging his golden inheritance
To restore St. Damien's Church, for a suffering leper,

Or, Christians captured by a sultan's Saracens. Today,
Again, Crusaders gather. Muslims bow to Mecca, mosques
Bleed; a scimitar moon bombs Jews near the Holy Sepulcher;
Christians bleed by the Tigris and Euphrates of antiquity.

Envisioning the seraph, Friars care for tombs, pilgrims,
Refugees from holy places like Bethlehem of the Crib,
Knights in white, in Jerusalem, places of The Passion
In Syria and Lebanon, Egyptian deserts. Dante

Wrote of St. Francis wedding the Lady Poverty.
We speak poetry St. Francis recited from the Psalms
As he prepared in early autumn to meet "Sister Death"
In the garden of St. Clare near Porziuncola.

His followers, the Franciscans in their sandals,
Minstrels of the catacombs, pray near battlefields;
Mystical St. Francis prayed to console the afflicted,
And, they say, he gleefully played two sticks like a violin

Among heavenly wildflowers, earthly as a song bird,
Cheerfully bleeding for Holy Communion, living in verse,
Preparing the dying with courtesy, the living for shipwrecks,
Relics, falcons, leaving a canticle—letting his *soul out of prison.*

—MICHAEL H. LYTHGOE

CLARE OF ASSISI

Patron Saint of Television

On Palm Sunday in 1212 A.D., had there been T.V.
she would have been in the panoramic crowd,
off to the side, a still-shot with a caption,
young and shy, too scared to step out for an olive branch,
so the bishop stepped out to her.

When she ran away to St. Francis,
he cut her hair, gave her her first
sackcloth tunic. It was a media event
without a media, a proud occasion
without the pride.

At her convent, she accepted no
possessions, no shoes or stockings
on her blistered feet. She slept penitently
and poorly on dirt, never tempted
her tongue with meat.

How she must pray now
for the remission of sins
of television, the daily soap opera
lives haloed by spotlights
in that square possession of possessions
hawking what the sponsors
sorely need us to need
in this eternal rerun.

—MARJORIE MADDOX

BLACK TRUFFLES

At the Hotel Subasio
one of the memorable meals
of my life: a plateful
of agnellotti, delicate packets
of pasta, stuffed with black truffles,

those dark earthy bits of countryside
that dissolve on the palate.

Later, as the sun goes down, we sit
on the veranda drinking the wine
my cousins gave me in Sicily.

The birds rise and fall
in the evening air, their
choreography hundreds of
years old. They are singing the songs
il poverello taught.

The earthquake has not yet
struck Assisi, but the tremors
are waiting. I savor
every moment.

I do not think of the future
or a return. We have done this well
once. It will only be later
when fresh black truffles
are unavailable and fragments
of the Giotto lie on tables
for reconstruction that I will hunger
for a second helping.

My cousins' wine can be replenished.
The next generation of birds
will repeat the aerial dances
of their ancestors and sing the songs
they learned, every generation
singing as if no one had ever
sung or danced like this before,

as if the discovery of black diamonds
had never happened before or will again,

but I will enter the earth
and rest like a unique truffle
until I begin to fall apart
like the fragrant earth, unexplored
by dogs or pigs, the rich dark earth
out of which we are all born.

—LEO LUKE MARCELLO

THE WOLF OF GUBBIO

Not the walls of the furled city,
through which he drifted like malign sleet,
nor every vigilance, could stop him.
He came and rent some poor soul
to morsels and ate him. There was no help
nearby, so St. Francis slogged
from Assisi to tame the wolf.
Sassetta painted this meeting.
The wolf, pert and teachable as Lassie,
has laid his licentious, vow-making right paw
in the saint's hand and meets with his

ochre eye the saint's chastening gaze.
The townspeople stand like a grove
and watch. Probably one of their faces
belonged to a patron who commissioned
Sassetta, but which face? Art remembers
a few things by forgetting many.
The wolf lived on in the nearby hills
but never ate, the story goes, another
citizen. Was Sassetta the last one,
then, to see on the piazza, like dropped
firewood, most of a leg and what may be
a forearm gnawed from both ends, lurid
with scarlet blood? None in the painting
looks at this carnage and bright waste,
nor thinks of the gnarled woods
in which the pewter-colored wolf
makes his huge home, nor measures with what work
each stone was prized from the furious ground
to build each house in Gubbio
and to lay a piazza atop the town
and to raise above it a tower.

—WILLIAM MATTHEWS

ASSISI

how you could give up
everything, everything

just like dying. of course
and the new birth naked

but not to want anything
or if you did, to deny it

deny your heart's
your body's dream, body

thrown into snow to slake
desire, to refuse it

brother body a donkey
beaten into silence

obedience. but we who
want you want things

too, ice cream and good
friendships at least, even

walking together in the
long penance parade

in the rich mild light
of this Italian town where

you were, are, every atom
scattered golden dust

—JANET McCANN

SONNET FROM ASSISI

Blind Francis, waiting to welcome Sister Death,
Worn though he was by ecstasies and fame,
Had heart for tune. With what remained of breath
He led his friars in canticles.

               Then came
Brother Elias, scowling, to his side,
Small-souled Elias, crying by book and candle,
This was outrageous! Had the monks no pride?
Music at deathbeds! Ah, the shame, the scandal!

Elias gave him sermons and advice
Instead of song; which simply proves once more
What things are sure this side of paradise:
Death, taxes, and the counsel of the bore.
Though we outwit the tithe, make death our friend,
Bores we have with us even to the end.

—PHYLLIS McGINLEY

ON A DAY IN AUGUST

These woods are too impersonal.
The deaf-and-dumb fields, waiting to be shaved of hay
Suffer the hours like an unexpected sea
While locusts fry their music in the sycamores.

But from the curdled places of the sky
(Where a brown wing hovers for carrion)
We have not seen the heaven-people come.

The clean, white saints, have they forgotten us?
Here we lie upon the earth

In the air of our dead grove
Dreaming some wind may come and kiss ourselves in the red
    eyes
With a pennyworth of mercy for our pepper shoulders.
And so we take into our hands the ruins
Of the words our minds have rent.

It is enough.
Our souls are trying to crawl out of our pores.
Our lives are seeping through each part of us like vinegar.
A sad sour death is eating the roots of our hair.

Yet doors of sanitary winds lie open in the clouds
To vistas of those laundries where the clean saints dwell:
If we could only view them from our slum!
But our dream has wandered away
And drowned in the din of the crickets' disconnected prayer.

Thus the grasses and the unemployed goldenrod
Go revel through our farm, and dance around the field.
The blue-black lights come shimmering upon the tar
Where kids made footprints in the melting way to Louisville.
And spooks come out of the road and walk the jagged heat
Like the time we found that drunkard lying still as murder
In the ditch behind the mill.

But you, Saint Clare,
We have been looking up your stairs all afternoon
Wanting to see you walking down some nimbus with your gentle
    friends.

Very well, clouds,
Open your purple bottles,
Cozen us never more with blowsy cotton:
But organize,

Summon the punishing lightning:
Spring those sudden gorgeous trees against the dark
Curtain of apocalypse you'll hang to earth, from heaven:
Let five white branches scourge the land with fire!
And when the first fat drops
Spatter upon the tin top of our church like silver dollars
And thoughts come bathing back to mind with a new life,
Prayer will become our new discovery

When God and His bad earth once more make friends.

—THOMAS MERTON

SONG TO SAINT FRANCIS

The Mother

As we do in the Gospel of the other divine Poor One, we should begin by praising you, Francis' mother, Maria of Italy.

Devout Madonna, you were the one whose womb made flesh this little swelling lump, so soft, who was to be called Francis of Assisi.

You'd come from Provence and traveled down into the valleys of Umbria. In youth, the gusty winds of your country had drummed at you; you'd walked through its biblical olive grove and vineyards. You'd carry a pitcher on your shoulders, like those women I watch descending from the lake, an amphora rubbing against their cheeks, shaped like flowers with double corollas. Because of the contrast of your grace with his coarseness, that coarse man, Pietro Bernardone, gazed at you.

We go down on our knees, genuflecting to kiss the saint's dust, but you, happy woman, had him lying at your breast thousands of nights; you filled him with the rich blood that in his heart became a tremendous charity; many of the lines of his body came, perhaps, from yours. (You could therefore be called "God's Chalice.") You taught him to speak, and from you, not from Bernadone, came that sweet accent in him, which gathered the birds around him, as if his words were birdseed and golden hemp.

You'd help him play; you'd round off the mound of blond sand that he'd flatten and build again. In this way you taught him forms in their various shapings, and you developed in him an eye that loved gracefulness. His desire to sing was something that came from you as well, from the songs with which you surrounded him when you had him on your knee, happy woman, able to give to a singing child a joyous tongue for a sorrowful world.

In the seven gentle years of his childhood, Christian woman, you guided him toward your Christ, like an imperceptible drop of honey through the ears, and you made your Christ as familiar to him as the creases in your neck...

And his humanity, his rapture for the human, wouldn't it have come from his watching you do the household chores, washing your feet, sweeping your dining room, good merchant's wife who wouldn't be too proud to do any of this?

I admire your equanimity when the hypocrites, annoyingly, tried to frighten you about young Francis' warm, youthful escapades. You'd hear them out calmly and then you'd smile, saying only that with time he would surely become a good son of the Lord.

And that day came, devout Madonna, but it brought you another trial: your Francis suddenly abandoned all of life's gifts, even his own sensibility, and set out to beg on the streets.

Shocked, the neighborhood women brought you this new scandal, though even it didn't disturb your deep sweetness.

The valleys have thanked you for those hands you provided,

so very loving, which freshened the countryside; the birds thank
you for that tongue with its new song, which you sent into the
wind; and the poor will always thank you for the Healer, for
Francis has been a loving bandage for a wounded world.

Now you are in heaven, next to Mary and near the mother
of Saint Julian, patron saint of hospitality, and you'll smile with
an eternal smile.

—GABRIELA MISTRAL

IN UMBRIA

For Daniel Long

The wrong assumption flirted with the possible:
A grave burst open,
St. Clare's body still in her nightdress
Flying in a vertical rush to Heaven,
Abandoning the stones speechless with sadness.
At first the woods were level, then unreal,
The stars alarmed by a wind shift, moonlight
Startled by the thrill of the extraordinary.
But soon the unexpected settles down,
Settles down, becoming ordinary
In landscapes compelled to tell a story—
Landscapes like this one seen from the tilted
Courtyard in front of the church in Assisi,
The hills peaceful with their fuzzy greenery,
Angels at rest who ask no questions,
And a sky that sails, finally, serenely.

In the church's glassed-in reliquary
A saint's bones give off neither a peculiar

Shining nor any semblance of the human.
Help is coming in this hospital
Of souls where first-aid never arrived
On time before; the holy bandages
Being folded now by hands of mercy
Will let that woman in black rise up
From her wounded knees, that gnarled old man
Believe in the sanctity of the uninjured.

Happy the monks strayed out of history
Walking forward toward the central fountain,
Dry, ornamental, surrounded by grasses.
Only the play of light on the hills,
Captures for good in religious paintings,
Serves as an emblem of the spiritual life
Of Umbria: three syllables of shade—
Or one—cast by a cypress tree
Alone in a field whose brush of thin
Shadow works the sundial of the day;
In this fief of the godly, art
And feeling are as intertwined
As orthodoxy and heresy.

"Far" and "down" are being redefined
In a medieval town up in the mountains.
Which is farther away: the valley
Floor invisible below or the distant
Hillside glimpsed in a haze of ozone—
The horizontal and the vertical
Having lost all meaning? The circle thrives—
The semicircle, rather—of the mountain
From whose rim the houses stacked in stone
Rise up again; a church and fountain

Domesticate a fortress of a town
Where the *gelateria* stays open late
and the park has the charm of the unnecessary.

So civil is it all
That one might be at a luncheon party
Attended by monks in a sunlit courtyard,
Clerics explaining to Swedish tourists
The history of the single Tintoretto
That has kept this monastery alive
Three hundred years. The wood of crucifixion
Lies everywhere about; its subject is either
Bred in the bone, in Umbria, or nothing:
The flowers are heavy with theology,
The birds fly by like Biblical quotations.
In all this shadowy world of sunlight,
In tiers and tiers of arranged hillsides,
Rays of evening fall on the earthworks.
The shades of Umbria are growing darker.

And what the dead have to say today
Is old, old as the hills, a phrase
Meaningless until one stares at these
Great slants of grave sites, reaching up
Always to the light, which the dead can't do,
Whose every particular is shelled to bone;
They say, "Our hearts, too, were full
Of sunlight once. Joy is in the shade.
Look at it. Look. It is beautiful."

—HOWARD MOSS

A SEPARATE WEAVE

A man makes money selling cloth
in the town square, then finds it missing
from his till. A son buys bricks to rebuild

a broken church, then flings down clothes
at his father's feet, a response to red silk
of riches, focus on wealth. The bishop

wraps the youth's naked body in his cloak.
It is over, father and son go separate ways,
the father cutting fabric and a fine profit,

the son renouncing himself from any bargain,
to fill the coffers of waifs and beggars.
Who would have thought the son would dare

to break the dangerous silence, shed
his father's shoes, refuse to possess? One
converges on skeins of returns in his material

world, the other on seamless garments of light
in the hollows, specters of peace
in the wrinkled hills, and a love so fervid

even a wolf lies at the pauper's dusty feet.

—KAY MULLEN

THE LIFE OF A SAINT

after Giotto

I. The Saint Leaves His Father's House
A boy walks out
onto the sun's bright stage.
The leaves are celebrating
the resurrection of birds,
the sky shouts hallelujah.
Nothing is more real than the dust
and the cobbled streets that shine
like water under his feet.
He is off to seek his fortune,
God, in the changing faces of the year.

A saint laughs
from the boy's throat;
his father's house becomes
a small reflection in his eyes.

II. The Saint's Dream
The saint gets up
in his skinny clothes.
His cave is cold and damp
as an April morning.
Even the sparrows
have found someplace to be warm.
The saint shivers to work:
he is performing penance for his eyes,
beheading all the flowers
that offend his sight.
He awakens suddenly on his feet

with his fists full of petals
and remembers his dazzling dream
of the night before.

He had entered the musical air
of the kingdom of heaven,
bared his head to the light
from five great thrones.
One throne,
fat cushions done in gold,
stood on a pedestal.

On the mountain
are only the wind
and the saint
but he hears
from the dust
like the voice of his mother,
long years dead,
someone saying,
"This was the chair of one
who would be holier than I."

III. Seducing the Saint
He was so pure
he only ate white flowers.
Nobody knew what his body
smelled like. His lips
opened and closed around prayers,
his thin skin was a bag
for blood and bones and a heart
that sang, beating,
the glory of God.

I went to him once
on a morning heavy with rain
to ask why my man
was a stranger to me
and why my womb worried
itself over and over to death,
and hardly had knelt
at his punctured feet
when the dove of the Lord
entered my belly
and opened his trembling wings.

It was a revelation.
Fire leapt like dogs
from my hair,
my mouth came alive,
I could read the secrets
in the scent of his robe,
birds tingled in my fingers,
I felt the shadows melt back
in my eyes.

Folding his hands
into his sleeves,
the saint arose.
"The way of woman
leads to darkness,"
he said, and threw himself
into that thicket there.
But the roses knew me
and drew in their thorns.
Their leaves caressed him
in my name, buds burst

into ecstatic blossom
all around him.

IV. The Saint Preaches
The saint has come back to town.
Everyone comes out.
His father's old retainers
whisper how he's changed.
He says he has a mistress now,
that his pride kisses the ground.
He seems so strange.
He carries his hunger
in a wooden bowl.

Some say they see his mistress,
that she's old
and wears rags. He says
he's been praying for years.
When he limps
through the streets
he leaves red footprints
for the rain to eat.
He looks as wild as the baptist,
everyone says, but they hang around
anyway when he starts to preach.

He's talking to something beyond them,
it seems, no, something so close
they'd forgotten to notice,
like their own good stink
or the beauty of kitchens.
When he opens his arms they think
birds fly out like coins.

He speaks a language they understand
but can't speak.
It sounds to them like singing,
like the melody of the wind
in the gray olive trees.

They hang around all day
and when they go home
it seems better,
as if they'd discovered salt.
They forget the dark
they're afraid of
and remember all night long
how the saint opened his wings
among the gathering birds,
how he opened his beak,
how he sang.

—MARILYN NELSON

ST. FRANCIS

In the flare of rose-bed
splendor he stands anew,
as if a plaster saint
could will himself to flesh
and bone and walk
from the neighbors'
backyard to mine. But no,
they came again last night,
devilish boys with Halloween
still up their sleeves.

Yet what they did was more
like love than any prank
they sprang and howled
before; and this, what's more
was done in silence softer
than the night they hid behind.

Today, no wind blows
and the spring sun is brilliant
over land and sea, an assurance
perhaps that what was done
the saint condoned with joy.

I've a mind to leave him there,
so elegantly oblivious
among the clouds of rose
and green, deeply involved
with the soft-sent coo

of a dove upon his wrist,
while the sun drinks holy
water from round his feet
like a blinding flock
of thirsty birds.

—ROGER PFINGSTON

A LETTER TO WILLIAM CARLOS WILLIAMS

Dear Bill,
When I search the past for you,
Sometimes I think you are like
St. Francis, whose flesh went out

Like a happy cloud from him,
And merged with every lover—
Donkeys, flowers, lepers, suns—
But I think you are more like
Brother Juniper, who suffered
All indignities and glories
Laughing like a gentle fool.
You're in the *Fioretti*
Somewhere, for you're a fool, Bill,
Like the Fool in Yeats, the term
Of all wisdom and beauty.
It's you, stands over against
Helen in all her wisdom,
Solomon in all his glory.

Remember years ago, when
I told you you were the first
Great Franciscan poet since
The Middle Ages? I disturbed
The even tenor of dinner.
Your wife thought I was crazy.
It's true, though. And you're 'pure,' too,
A real classic, though not loud
About it—a whole lot like
The girls of the Anthology.
Not like strident Sappho, who
For all her grandeur, must have
Had endemetriosis,
But like Anyte, who says
Just enough, softly, for all
The thousands of years to remember.

It's a wonderful quiet
You have, a way of keeping

Still about the world, and its
Dirty rivers, and garbage cans,
Red wheelbarrows glazed with rain,
Cold plums stolen from the icebox,
And Queen Anne's lace, and day's eyes,
And leaf buds bursting over
Muddy roads, and splotched bellies
With babies in them, and Cortes
And Malinche on the bloody
Causeway, the death of the flower world.

Nowadays, when the press reels
With chatterboxes, you keep still,
Each year a sheaf of stillness,
Poems that have nothing to say,
Like the stillness of George Fox,
Sitting still under the cloud
Of all the world's temptation,
By the fire, in the kitchen,
In the Vale of Beavor. And
The archetype, the silence
Of Christ, when he paused a long
Time and then said, 'Thou sayest it.'

Now in a recent poem you say,
'I who am about to die.'
Maybe this is just a tag
From the classics, but it sends
A shudder over me. Where
Do you get that stuff, Williams?
Look at here. The day will come
When a young woman will walk
By the lucid Williams River,

Where it flows through an idyllic
News from Nowhere sort of landscape,
And she will say to her children,
'Isn't it beautiful? It
Is named after a man who
Walked here once when it was called
The Passaic, and was filthy
With the poisonous excrements
Of sick men and factories.
He was a great man. He knew
It was beautiful then, although
Nobody else did, back there
In the Dark Ages. And the
Beautiful river he saw
Still flows in his veins, as it
Does in ours, and flows in our eyes,
And flows in time, and makes us
Part of it, and part of him.
That, children, is what is called
A sacramental relationship.
And that is what a poet
Is, children, one who creates
Sacramental relationships
That last always.'

　　　　With love and admiration,
　　　　Kenneth Rexroth.

—KENNETH REXROTH

TRAVELING LIGHT

Only few have known the joy of traveling light
though many think it's happiness
they recognize glowing in the humble heart
of the homeless' scrappy campfire, and love
he feels for the few things in the bundle
he clings to and totes over one shoulder.

On a busy street toward the eastern edge of the city
there is one of the many shanty towns
basking in the sun and flies, embarrassing to those
who live in heavy suburban houses that stand nearby
within high walls, broken glass and barbed wire
protecting the cars, appliances and silverware.

The shanty town is a mess of stones, boards, old
tires, and laundry flapping in the dust and smoke.
There too every little dwelling is weighted down
with things the poor have collected from dumps
and philanthropic gifts that others make of old
and useless things they themselves no longer want.

The few who knew tried to convince us of the joy:
Gandhi, barefoot in a loincloth and a sheet;
Francis, standing naked as a bird
before a scandalized cathedral; and Jesus Himself,
sending out the twelve, admonishing them to take
neither shoes, staff, nor extra shirt on their journey.

The city lies sad and still at the end of the day,
stuffed full and weighted down with heavy things,
aching to travel but unable to get up and go.
With a tin cup amid the rush of urgent feet,

a beggar is singing a crude and lonesome song
about the terrible joy of traveling light.

—JAMES MILLER ROBINSON

OUR LORD CHRIST: OF ORDER

Set love in order, thou that lovest me,
Never was virtue out of order found;
And though I fill thy heart desirously,
By thine own virtue I must keep My ground;
When to My love thou dost bring charity;
Even she must come with order girt and gown'd,
Look how the trees are bound
To order, bearing fruit;
And by one thing compute,
In all things earthly order's grace or gain.

All earthly things I had the making of
Were numbered and were measured then by Me;
And each was order'd to its end by Love,
Each kept, through order, clean for ministry.
Charity most of all, when known enough,
Is of her very nature orderly.
Lo, now! what heat in thee,
Soul, can have bred this rout?
Thou putt'st all order out,
Even this love's heat must be its curb and rein.
        (after St. Francis)

—DANTE GABRIEL ROSSETTI

CANDLEMAS DAWN QUESTION: IS THERE POETRY PAST FORTY

If you're a poet at 20, it's because you're 20; if you're a poet at 40, it's because you're a poet.
—Joel Oppenheimer

At 6 a.m. I punch out and head home.
At ten below boots quack over new snow.
I stop under a street light to admire
the meteorological phenomena I heard
described on the news—ice crystals
in the air make light appear to shine up.

Passing 40 one is attentive to reversals,
no time to hide light under a bushel,
no time to be afraid of the shadow
who lives in a cyst under your heart
where cells with no replacements go.

I fight to keep from drifting out past
ritual where habit practices a haughty tremor
and doggerel thumps out each year
rhyming all the tales old wives tell—
whiskers, humpback, a thickening.

St. Francis presides over the parking lot,
his outspread hands filled with snow.
The light flies up from him.
Even old wives know there is more
than time clocks, money, the cold walk home.

Light a candle or curse the dark.
It's a measure of the grace
we take our grain of salt with.

—HELEN RUGGIERI

NEGLIGIBLE

The ant, brief as a second,
lone scout of dew and peony petals,
black on cream. Easy to pluck,
and a trifling crunch
under foot.

The dust-mite also,
invisible to the eye, invading
pillows, mattresses, with her
generations—fuse for my
explosive allergies.

Assumed: that we will stand in awe
of larger things, like the bull-dozer
tearing the ancient cedars
from the lot down the road. Or a bomb.
Or the oceans. Or the expanding universe.

But let us up-end our thoughts:
What matchstick of vexation
lights the slow fuse of rancor.
How like a parasite
it eats at our gut.

And how one moment's
catalytic radiance (think: St. Clare,
at Portiuncula) tilts, overturns the universe,
plants our feet on heaven's
widening threshold.

—LUCI SHAW

CARELESS FLYING

1

I have been considering
the ravens, who live
without worrying
and have no bins or barns

and use no reaping machines.
Yet they are fed well—their bodies
sleek, gloved in black silk.
With what a minor tempest

they startle and settle,
yet they are the poets of motion.
Like folk songs their wings wheel
and hover, careless

as falcons. I am their
anxious scribe, listening myself
into their coarse
cries, storing the separate

notes in small black spaces
at the back of my skull.
God, if I were a bird I think
I would stop worrying.

Enough to wear, to eat. And one
more hour of life is, he says,
not worth the care. So, I'm
a young bird. Nested in down,

I think I will rest in a
dream of flight all night,
waking at the gold call of the sun
from the world's lip.

2
Francis, you could name me
your small sister.
You weren't a bird either
but you would know how to fold

your hands around my minor
warmth, then toss me, your arms
splayed, and let the air
catch me easy as feathers.

Watching ravens rise to God,
black specks moving on gold
ladders, gave you enough wonder
it took all of your life

to revel in. Your praise
escaped often to heaven, your eyes
following. Eventually you yourself
learned to fly, lifted by birds.

—LUCI SHAW

SAINT FRANCIS IN NORTH ZULCH AT 1 A.M.

for Janet

There's a light on in my neighbors' screen porch
and a large cardboard box on the second
best table stored out there. Judy showed me
the quivering ball of baby possums
asleep in it this afternoon. She's the
Wildlife Rehabilitator for the whole

county, and though she prefers to work with
deer, she only recently released
a skunk she'd kept a year. Two armadillo
(who refused to leave) inhabit the crawl space
beneath her house, and a hare lives in it
she's never seen (only its droppings)
for which she leaves out food religiously.
In fact, her whole yard's full of feeders, but
the focal point's the concrete statue
of Saint Francis, near the small bare patch where
the toad house was till Judy removed it
(after killing two snakes in seven days.)

She's pacing the porch with a clutch of possums
wrapped in a frayed towel, pressed to her breast.
I can hear her voice gravelling faintly
and guess she's talking to Francis again
(between long drags on her cigarette)
about how she wishes he'd hurry up
and find a replacement at this post,
about her poor general health—
how the diabetes is getting her down
and the anti-depressants are making
her sick, and her feet are swelling—
how she didn't even feel the piercing wound
she got, mowing the side lawn in her slippers.
How she doesn't care much for possums herself,
'but these are just helpless babies, so if you can
put a good word in the LORD's ear, please do.'

I'm still staring as she puts the bundle back
and adjusts the heat lamp over the box
before leaving the porch. Now I can't sleep

because I still hear a voice, intoning
through pin oak leaves in an ancient tongue:
"Pax et bonum, didelphes virginianae."

—OLYMPIA SIBLEY

FRANCESCO AND CLARE

It was there, in the little town
On top of the mountain, they walked,
Francesco and Chiara,
That's who they were, that's what
They told themselves—a joke, their joke
About two saints, failed lovers held apart
From the world of flesh, Francis and Clare,
Out walking the old city, two saints,
Sainted ones, holy, held close to the life...
Poverty, the pure life, the one
Life for Franziskus and Klara,
Stalwarts given
To the joys of God in heaven
And on earth, Mother, praising Brother Sun
And sister Moon; twin saints, unified
In their beauty as one, Francisco and Clara,
A beauty said of God's will and word, bestowed
And polished by poverty, François
With Claire, the chosen poverty, the true
Poverty that would not be their lives...

And they took their favorite names, Clare and Francesco,
Walking the streets of stone the true saints
Walked, watching as the larks swirled
Above the serene towers, the larks

Francesco once described as the color
Of goodness, that is, of the earth, of the dead . . .
Larks who'd not seek for themselves any extravagant
Plumage, humble and simple, God's birds
Twirling and twisting up the pillowing air...
And Francesco said to Clare, *Oh little plant I love,*
My eyes are almost blind with Brother Sun...tell me,
Who hides inside God's time...?
And Clare, rock of all Poor Clares, stood
In the warm piazza overlooking the valley, weary,
Her shoulder bag sagging from the weight
Of her maps and books, and said across the rain-slick
Asphalt of the parking lot, to the poor bird climbing
The wheel of sky it always had loved best,
Dear lark, dear saint, all my kisses on your nest!

Assisi

—DAVID ST. JOHN

A CANTICLE TO CARRY AWAY

for my friends at Our Lady of Angels

I.
Behind the gym, beyond the purple rhododendron,
where ivy spills over stones, JESUS IS CONDEMNED TO
     DEATH.
I know it was I who condemned, and yet in this place,
in this pocket of time, I have found some peace—
just enough to nibble from, a reminder, a crumb.

I listened, little rain fell, and St. Francis said, *May*
the power of your love, O Lord, fiery and sweet as honey,
wean my heart from all that is under heaven, so that I
may die for love of your love, who were so good
as to die for love of my love.

II.

Where laurel reaches and the first bench waits,
I turn around once and gaze: JESUS RECEIVES HIS CROSS.
And Francis said, *Brother fire, God made you*
beautiful; I pray you be courteous with me.
I remember how when I closed my eyes, the bees
gathered at the lip of the hive board…the affectionate
cat followed me through tall grass…and I went beyond,
where old apple trees kneeled down, offering
all they had to the sun and the south. And I remember
how in my dream at the little portion, a voice asked
"What about the house?" And in answer, with two
words, a crow woke me, and then a song sparrow
spilled a scale, and the answer was this place
as it will always be.

III.

Go down now, into the wood, the thick green shade
where JESUS FALLS THE FIRST TIME. At my feet, young
holly, young fern spring out of the earth. I remember
how a crow on the golden cross called down to me
and I was far from my home, but my pocket of peace
was a hum of bees, a blur of tall grass, frogs calling
in their ravine. A distant siren, the train pulling heavy
across the river far, a car rushing somewhere beyond
the hedge all reminded me of the world. Here, a room
where I settled on the ground beneath the purple plum

to watch a five-point star flower suspended on a
filament of web turn slowly in the smallest wind.
And Francis said to the birds, *Little sisters, if you
have now had your say, it is time that I also
should be heard.*

IV.
JESUS MEETS HIS BLESSED MOTHER above the
        moss-roofed
hut where the towhee questions, "See? See?" In solitude,
I see, I feel, and my mother throngs to mind. And once
I saw a crow fly out from the flowering cherry
pursued by a jay, and the jay pursued by a small
brown bird—all busy like me on a web of errands
in the world. But Francis gave up all riches
save these: a love of the beautiful, a sense
of humor, and a habit for courtesy and praise.

V.
Remember St. Francis small and intent as a knee-high
boy in the contortions of old juniper? Now, here, I
sit in the grotto of red stone, where Indian peach arches
over the path, and SIMON HELPS JESUS TO CARRY HIS
        CROSS.
What will console me—a crow far away, a drop of rain?
They say that in a court there are one king and a thousand
courtiers, but in the world of Francis, he is the one
courtier serving a thousand kings and queens.
What do you need that I might give?

VI.
And someone said how Francis looked into the eyes
of every person with supreme individual interest—
he could never see a crowd, only each soul present.

Here, mosquito whines. How small can mercy go?
Kinglets chatter, and the long aria of the winter wren.
What if our guide for change came simply to this:
What would be best for the birds of this place?
Salal always in good humor, slender hazel wands
reaching for light: VERONICA WIPES THE FACE OF
    JESUS.

VII.
Small-leafed spangle of green, red huckleberry, and the fern
called licorice root (bitter if you bite down hard, but sweet
if you nibble gently): JESUS FALLS THE SECOND TIME.

VIII.
And Francis said, *If we had any possessions,*
we should need weapons and laws to defend them.
My shadow moving on a tree, serviceberry over my head:
JESUS CONSOLES THE HOLY WOMEN. He turned to
    them
and offered his spirit. And I remembered in the library
at night how I was consoled, when the automatic sensor
would click off, and in darkness I would stand and raise
my arms in praise to bring the light back blooming.

IX.
And someone pointed out how it was for those with
Francis—how the vow of poverty opened a great
freedom, for his followers should be like little fishes
swimming in and out of the net of trouble in the world. Here,
I begin to climb. The path will turn. Someone planted pines
from Italy. Someone planted Oregon sword fern, spruce.
JESUS FALLS THE THIRD TIME.

X.
Remember beyond the garden, where the chard had bolted,
asparagus become a forest, and beyond: dead maple
with one living branch. Here in the wood, I gaze on
snowberry, twisted stalk, thimbleberry, wild rose trembling:
JESUS IS STRIPPED OF HIS GARMENTS. And I
     remember how
Francis drew images in the snow and cried out to the devil,
These will suffice for wife and children.

XI.
I remember at supper, when I lowered my gaze
I heard all about me the light of discovery in voices
of fellow pilgrims: "It was a subtle kind of redemption...
my grandmother was a notorious hypochondriac:
she lived 96 years without a single day of good health...
and so I kept a journal of my joys, and just as pain
teaches the body what not to do, so joy taught me
what I should do, and I lived by that and quit my job."
Down here, in the wood, vanilla leaf, Oregon grape,
young cedar, old fir: JESUS IS NAILED TO THE CROSS.
And the screensaver said: *You can be trusted*
with God's abundance. And sometimes our abundance
is pain.

XII.
When I am old, I will know how steep the world can be.
But someone told me how for Francis, the whole work
of the mystic was to become more cheerful and humane.
Here stands trillium, young maples coming up
through gravel at my feet: JESUS EXPIRES ON THE
     CROSS.
Living dogwood slender and tall, wild cherry, and rue.

Within me, like the rude stone chapel of the little portion
housed in the great basilica, this time will stand.

XIII.
Who made ivy eager? Who made hawthorn cruel?
JESUS IS TAKEN FROM THE CROSS. And when they
    carried
Francis home, it is told how he who had become a vagabond
for a vision cried out to his friends, *Never give up*
this place. If you would go anywhere or make any pilgrimage,
return always to your home. For this is the holy house of
God. And I knew I would never give up this place
from my heart. I would carry on every road the stations
of this path, the leaves and the sunlight and rain, the silence
and the calls of birds, the hum of our bees, the old
apples kneeling deep in tall grass. I will never
give up this place from the work I will be.

XIV.
And the wind came through the forest everywhere,
touching each leaf in turn, embracing all of us
gently, simply, as the spirit moves through a gathering
in silence, as music moves, an idea waking the young.
Here in the wood, it is time to stand, to turn east:
two maples joined at the hip. My brother, my sister,
it is time we go out into the light. Old hemlock of
many little cones: JESUS IS LAID IN THE SEPULCHRE.
Now shield my eyes. Go forth.

—KIM STAFFORD

ST. FRANCIS IN ECSTASY (BELLINI)

In the morning, the voices wake him.
A crack in the rock fixes the light.
He looks west with the egret and donkey.
A cluster of copper-green leaves
shakes above the fissure.
He forgets his sandals by the bed,
his open book on the table.

—SUE STANDING

FROM "LOCKSLEY HALL, 60 YEARS AFTER"

...Are we devils? are we men?
Sweet St. Francis of Assisi, would that he were here again,
He that in his Catholic wholeness used to call the very flowers
Sisters, brothers—and the beasts—whose pains are hardly less
    than ours!

—ALFRED LORD TENNYSON

AFTER-STRAIN

(from "Ode to the Setting Sun")

Now with wan ray that other sun of Song
    Sets in the bleakening waters of my soul:
One step, and lo! the Cross stands gaunt and long
    'Twixt me and yet bright skies, a presaged dole.

Even so, O Cross! thine is the victory.
  Thy roots are fast within our fairest fields;
Brightness may emanate in Heaven from thee,
  Here thy dread symbol only shadow yields.

Of reapèd joys thou art the heavy sheaf
  Which must be lifted, though the reaper groan;
Yea, we may cry till Heaven's great ear be deaf,
  But we must bear thee, and must bear alone.

Vain were a Simon; of the Antipodes
  Our night not borrows the superfluous day.
Yet woe to him that from his burden flees,
  Crushed in the fall of what he cast away.

Therefore, O tender Lady, Queen Mary,
  Thou gentleness that dost enmoss and drape
The Cross's rigorous austerity,
  Wipe thou the blood from wounds that needs must gape.

'Lo, though suns rise and set, but crosses stay,
  I leave thee ever,' saith she, 'light of cheer.'
'Tis so: yon sky still thinks upon the Day,
  And showers aërial blossoms on his bier.

Yon cloud with wrinkled fire is edgèd sharp;
  And once more welling through the air, ah me!
How the sweet viol plains him to the harp,
  Whose pangèd sobbings throng tumultuously.

Oh, this Medusa-pleasure with her stings!
  This essence of all suffering, which is joy!
I am not thankless for the spell it brings,
  Though tears must be told down for the charmed toy.

No; while soul, sky, and music bleed together,
    Let me give thanks even for those griefs in me,
The restless windward stirrings of whose feather
    Prove them the brood of immortality.

My soul is quitted of death-neighbouring swoon,
    Who shall not slake her immitigable scars
Until she hear 'My sister!' from the moon,
    And take the kindred kisses of the stars.

—FRANCIS THOMPSON

FRANCISCUS CHRISTIFICATUS

Thief that has leaped Heaven's star-spiked wall
Christ's exultant bacchanal!
Wine-smears on thy hand and foot
Of the Vine that struck its root
Deep in Virgin soil, and was
Trained against the reared Cross:
Nay, thy very side its stain
Hath, to make it redly plain
How in the wassail quaffed full part
That flown vintager, thy heart.
Christ in blood stamps Himself afresh
On thy Veronical-veil of flesh.

Lovers, looking with amaze on
Each other, would be that they gaze on:
So for man's love God would be
Man, and man for His love He:
What God in Christ, man has in thee.
God gazed on man and grew embodied,

Thou, on Him gazing, turn'st engodded!
But though he held thy brow-spread tent
His little Heaven above Him bent,
The sceptering reed suffices thee,
Which smote Him into sovereignty.

Thou who thoughtest thee too low
For His priest, thou shalt not so
'Scape Him and unpriested go!
In thy hand thou wouldst not hold Him,
In thy flesh though shalt enfold Him;
Bread would not change into Him...ah see!
How He doth change Himself to thee!

—FRANCIS THOMPSON

STEWARD

The St. Francis we picked up
along Route 460 in 1987 stands here
in the second yard of his career.
I inherited him when you left,
though it was you who decided
we needed him in the first place.
Now, fifteen years later, the bottom half
of his cassock is turning chalky pale
from the ministrations of Brother Sun
and Brothers Wind and Air,
all the agencies of weather's moods.

He might be addressing the starlings
perched on the hum of utility wires,
foraging over the lawn—or cardinals

who seem to prefer the bird bath,
a jay triumphant at the feeder.
They don't appear to be listening
as the old accounts tell us they did
centuries ago. Still, he stands there
with boundless patience, a dove
cradled solicitously in his arms
as if his piety could make a difference
here in this world he wasn't born to.

Cars and trucks speed past—the street
no more than a hundred feet away—
their incessant hum drowning the hush
of this city yard. "Be praised, O Lord,
for Sister Death," is what he is said
to have sung at his life's end.
There is nothing he can do.

—ERIC TRETHEWEY

TO SAINT FRANCIS

Saint Francis, patron of zoologists and ornithologists
why does the
bison groan
deer bleat
fox yelp
squirrel spatter
blackbird whistle
eagle scream
quail quail
mockingbird shout

wood-cock snore
coalmouse ring
dove coo
fieldfare squeak
corncrake grind
jackdaw jack
swallow cheep
crane struck
bustard hiss
man speak sing and howl
only butterflies have big eyes
and so much unspeakable silence
that does not answer any questions.

—JAN TWARDOWSKI
(TRANSLATED BY KAZIMIERZ AND JUSTYAN BRAUN)

THE LADY POVERTY

I met her on the Umbrian hills,
Her hair unbound, her feet unshod:
As one whom secret glory fills
She walked, alone with God.

I met her in the city street:
Oh, changed was all her aspect then!
With heavy eyes and weary feet
She walked alone, with men.

—EVELYN UNDERHILL

RIVER

One day, in November, I stood in an open field
after walking in a cemetery in New Oxford, PA.
It was a cold day and it had just stopped raining
as a river of birds passed over, five, ten minutes,
an endless black ribbon of small birds stretched
horizon to horizon. Nearby, Saint Francis stood,
a half-scale likeness at least, with a small deer.

In the cemetery there was one particular stone,
for twin brothers, that told a story of disparate
fortunes in a few words and dates. One died
a child, the other lived many years, and there
between them, between the years apart in this
small town, they were joined by a simple stone
the long-lived brother purchased for them to share.

—SEAN WEBB

ST. FRANCIS EINSTEIN OF THE DAFFODILS

On the first visit of Professor Einstein to
the United States in the spring of 1921.

"Sweet land"
at last!
out of the sea—
the Venusremembering wavelets
rippling with laughter—
freedom
for the daffodils!

—in a tearing wind
that shakes

the tufted orchards—
Einstein, tall as a violet
in the lattice-arbor corner
is tall as
a blossomy peartree

A Samos, Samos
dead and buried. Lesbia
a black cat in the freshturned
garden. All dead.
All flesh they sung
is rotten
Sing of it no longer—

Side by side young and old
take the sun together—
maples, green and red
yellowbells
and the vermillion quinceflower
together—

The peartree
with foetid blossoms
sways its high topbranches
with contrary motions
and there are both pinkflowered
and coralflowered peachtrees
in the bare chickenyard
of the old negro
with white hair who hides
poisoned fish-heads
here and there
where stray cats find them—
find them

Spring days
swift and mutable
winds blowing four ways
hot and cold
shaking the flowers—

Now the northeast wind
moving in fogs leaves the grass
cold and dripping. The night
is dark. But in the night
the southeast wind approaches.
The owner of the orchard
lies in bed
with open windows
and throws off his covers
one by one.

—WILLIAM CARLOS WILLIAMS

BENEDICTION

St. Anthony went to the mouth of the river by the sea,
and began to call the fishes in God's name.
    —Little Flowers of St. Francis

Evening genuflects,
While I kneel at the creek's edge
Watching bluegill rise to tossed petals,
Wanting to write words, right as rain
Smooth as skipped stones—
And release them when the aim
And balance are right.
Fish rushing to the rings of forever

As they must have done
To the poor man of Padua's blessing,
While gathering prayers in the dark.

—BROTHER RICK WILSON, T.O.R.

ST. FRANCIS AND THE LEPER

> *Once we understand the natural history of leprosy,*
> *it becomes clear that a diagnosis of tuberculoid leprosy best*
> *accounts for Francis' illness. His stigmata can be understood*
> *as the wounds of a man who became a leper precisely because*
> *of his love for the Crucified Leper.*
> —Schazlein & Sumasy

The leper that I've shunned
Is the Christ I'm asked to face
On this journey I've begun.

The stench had left me stunned,
His countenance I debased,
This leper that I've shunned.

My world has come undone
By the miracle of His grace
On this journey I've begun.

For the riches that are won
Are gathered in embrace
From the leper that I've shunned.

With wounds that leave me numb
Brother Ass is laid to waste
On the journey I've begun.

So I no longer run
Or live my life in haste
Fearing the leper I once shunned.

Though I burn with Brother Sun
It's His passion that I trace
In the hug, that kiss, His face:

See the leper I've become
As I live a life displaced
On my journey to the Son.

—BROTHER RICK WILSON, T.O.R.

CONTRITION IN ASSISI

So much, so much money
I had to raise to travel to the sanctuary of penury.

Here, o Seraphim singer, every stone confesses you.
Human heart is harder, so turn it into stone.

From all over the world, bored lords and ladies arrive by train
In sleeping-cars to kiss the hand of your spouse Poverty.

In a hotel next to the church where your body reposes
Waiters bring resplendent ice-creams on silver platters.

Sweeter the chill of your tears, better the bread of your alms!
Well-fed, we admire your belly that often was empty.

Where your blood's drops were food for the birds,
Today a cook murders your humble brother, chicken.

We parade vanity clothed in most costly fabrics
Where you walked naked, the son of a textile merchant.

Your basilicas we enter with hearts full of devotion,
And exchange our dollars at the Banco di Spirito Santo.

Like wolves we lie in wait for our neighbor's trouble
In the spot where you made peace with the wolf of Gubbio.

O good mediator of all who are beaten,
Calm human hearts as you calmed the doves.

Stretch your bleeding hand, pierced by God's stigmata,
Make peace eternal between us and the world.

—JÓZEF WITTLIN (TRANSLATED BY KAZIMIERZ AND
JUSTYNA BRAUN)

FROM "THE CUCKOO AT LAVERNIA"

Oft have I heard the Nightingale and Thrush
Blending as in a common English grove
Their love-songs; but, where'er my feet might
    roam,
Whate'er assemblages of new and old,
Strange and familiar, might beguile the way,
A gratulation from that vagrant Voice
Was wanting;—and most happily till now.

    For see, Lavernia! mark the far-famed Pile,
High on the brink of that precipitous rock,
Implanted like a Fortress, as in truth
It is, a Christian Fortress, garrisoned
In faith and hope, and dutiful obedience,
By a few Monks, a stern society,
Dead to the world and scorning earth-born joys.
Nay—though the hopes that drew, the fears that
    drove,

St. Francis, far from Man's resort, to abide
Among these sterile heights of Apennine,
Bound him, nor, since he raised yon House, have
    ceased
To bind his spiritual Progeny, with rules
Stringent as flesh can tolerate and live;
His milder Genius (thanks to the good God
That made us) over those severe restraints
Of mind, that dread heart-freezing discipline,
Doth sometimes here predominate, and works
By unsought means for gracious purposes;
For earth through heaven, for heaven, by changeful
    earth,
Illustrated, and mutually endeared.

    Rapt though He were above the power of sense,
Familiarly, yet out of the cleansed heart
Of that once sinful being overflowed
On sun, moon, stars, the nether elements,
And every shape of creature they sustain,
Divine affections; and with beast and bird
(Stilled from afar—such marvel story tells—
By casual outbreak of his passionate words,
And from their own pursuits in field or grove
Drawn to his side by look or act of love
Humane, and virtue of his innocent life)
He wont to hold companionship so free,
So pure, so fraught with knowledge and delight,
As to be likened in his Followers' minds
To that which our first Parents, ere the fall
From their high state darkened the Earth with fear,
Held with all kinds in Eden's blissful bowers.

—WILLIAM WORDSWORTH

UMBRIAN DREAMS

Nothing is flat-lit and tabula rasaed in Charlottesville,
Umbrian sackcloth,
        stigmata and *Stabat mater,*
A sleep and a death away,
Night, and a sleep and a death away—
Light's frost-fired and Byzantine here,
        aureate, beehived,
Falling in Heraclitean streams
Through my neighbor's maple trees.
There's nothing medieval and two-dimensional in our town,
October in full drag, Mycenaean masked and golden lobed.

Like Yeats, however, I dream of a mythic body,
Feathered and white, a landscape
        horizoned and honed as an anchorite.
(Iacopo, hear me out, St. Francis, have you a word for me?)
Umbrian lightfall, lambent and ichorous, mists through my
        days,
As though a wound, somewhere and luminous,
        flickered and went out,
Flickered and went back out—
So weightless the light, so stretched and pained,
It seems to ooze, and then not ooze, down from that one hurt.
You doubt it? Look. Put your finger there. No, there. You see?

—CHARLES WRIGHT

THE FOURTH LETTER TO BLESSED AGNES OF PRAGUE

To her who is half of her soul and the special shrine of her heart's deepest love, to the illustrious Queen and Bride of the Lamb, the eternal King: to the Lady Agnes, her most dear mother, and, of all the others, her favorite daughter. Clare, an unworthy servant of Christ and a *useless* handmaid (Luke 17:10) of His handmaids in the monastery of San Damiano of Assisi: health and [a prayer] that she may sing *a new song* (Revelation 14:3) with the other most holy virgins before the throne of God and the Lamb and *follow the Lamb wherever He may go* (Revelation 14:4).

O mother and daughter, spouse of the King of all ages, if I have not written to you as often as your soul—and mine as well— desire and long for, do not wonder or think that the fire of love for you glows with less delight in the heart of your mother. No, this is the difficulty: the lack of messengers and the obvious dangers of the roads. Now, however, as I write to your love, I rejoice and exault with you in the *joy of the Spirit* (1 Thessalonians 1:6), O spouse of Christ, because, since you have totally abandoned the vanities of this world, like the other most holy virgin, Saint Agnes, you have been marvelously espoused to *the spotless Lamb, Who takes away the sins of the world* (1 Peter 1:19, John 1:29).

Happy, indeed is she
    to whom it is given to share in this sacred banquet
    so that she might cling with all her heart
    to Him
        Whose beauty all the blessed hosts of heaven unceasingly
        admire
        Whose affection excites

Whose contemplation refreshes,
Whose kindness fulfills,
Whose delight refreshes,
Whose remembrance delightfully shines,
By Whose frangrance the dead are revived,
Whose glorious vision will bless
   all the citizens of the heavenly Jerusalem:
      which, since it is the splendor of eternal glory, is
      the brilliance of eternal light
   and the mirror without blemish.

Gaze upon that mirror each day, O Queen and Spouse of Jesus
Christ, and continually study your face within it, that you may
adorn yourself within and without with beautiful robes, covered,
as is becoming the daughter and most chaste bride of the Most
High King....

Look at the border of this mirror, that is, the poverty of Him
Who has placed in a manger and wrapped in swaddling clothes.

         O Marvelous humility
         O astonishing poverty!
         The King of angels,
      the Lord of heaven and earth,
         is laid in a manger!

Then, at the surface of the mirror, consider the holy humility,
the blessed poverty, the untold labors and burdens that He
endured for the redemption of the whole human race. Then in
the depth of that same mirror, contemplate the ineffable charity
that led Him to suffer on the wood of the Cross and to die there
the most shameful kind of death.
      Therefore,
         that mirror,

suspended on the wood of the Cross,
urged those who passed by to consider, saying:

"All you who passed by the way,
look and see if there is any suffering
like my suffering!"

Let us respond
with one voice,
with one spirit,
to Him crying and grieving Who said:

"Remembering this over and over
leaves my soul downcast within me!"

...In this contemplation, may you remember your poor little
mother, knowing that I have inscribed the happy memory of you
on the tablets of my heart (Proverbs 3:3), holding you dearer than
all others....

Farewell, my dearest daughter, to you and your daughters until
we meet at the throne of *the glory of the great God* (Titus 2:13),
and desire [this] for us.

Inasmuch as I can, I recommend to your charity the bearers of
this letter, our dearly beloved Brother Amatus, *beloved of God*
and men (Sirach 45:1), and Brother Bonaugura. Amen.

—SAINT CLARE OF ASSISI

THE CANTICLE OF THE CREATURES

Most High, all-powerful, good Lord,
Yours are *the praises, the glory,* and *the honor and all blessing,*
To You alone, Most High, do they belong,
and no human is worthy to mention Your name.

Praised be You, my *Lord*, with all *Your creatures*,
    especially Sir Brother Sun,
    Who is the day and through whom You give us light.
And he is beautiful and radiant with great splendor;
    And bears a likeness of You, Most High One.
Praised be You, my Lord, through Sister Moon and the stars,
    In heaven You formed them clear and precious and
      beautiful.
Praised be You, my Lord, through Brother Wind,
    and through the air, cloudy and serene, and every kind of
      weather,
    through whom You give sustenance to Your creatures.
Praised be You, my Lord, through Sister *Water*,
    Who is very useful and humble and precious and chaste.
Praised be You, my Lord, through Brother *Fire*,
    Through whom *You light the night*,
    and he is beautiful and playful and robust and strong.
Praised be You my Lord, through our Sister Mother *Earth*,
    Who sustains and governs us,
    And who produces various fruit with colored flowers and
      herbs.

Praised be You, my Lord, through those who give pardon for
Your
    love,
    and bear infirmity and tribulation.
Blessed are those who endure in peace
    for by You, Most High, shall they be crowned....

Praise and *bless* my *Lord* and give Him thanks
    And serve him with great humility.

—Saint Francis of Assisi

Notes on Contributors

Dante Alighieri, the renowned Florentine creator of *The Divine Comedy*, was born in 1265 and died in 1321. His work is probably the most widely read and translated of all medieval writers'. We have used Longfellow's translation.

Jan Lee Ande's first book, *Instructions for Walking on Water*, won the 2000 Snyder Prize from Ashland Poetry Press. Her second book, *Reliquary*, won the 2002 X.J. Kennedy Poetry Prize from Texas Review Press. She comes from a long line of Anglican clergy, was initiated into Tibetan Buddhism and later joined a Roman Catholic community. Besides an M.A. in Asian studies and a Ph.D. in history of consciousness, she has an M.F.A. in poetry from San Diego State University.

Father Murray Bodo is a Franciscan priest. His poems have appeared in *The Paris Review, Western Humanities Review, Cincinnati Poetry Review, Mystics Quarterly, Cistercian Studies, Tracks (Dublin), The Cord* and *St. Anthony Messenger*. His latest collection of poems is *The Earth Moves at Midnight* (St. Anthony Messenger Press, 2003).

John Bowers is a poet and playwright who teaches at St. Francis University in Joliet, Illinois; he has a Ph.D. in renaissance literature. He lives in Joliet with his wife Linda and his son Nick. He has recently received a grant to write a play about Saint Francis and is at work on it.

Roman Brandstaetter, 1906-1987, a Polish poet, was born and raised a Jew. He converted to Catholicism. Besides writing original poetry, he produced highly regarded translations from Hebrew, including the Psalms and other books of the Bible. He wrote two longer poems about Saint Francis: *The Assisi Chronicles* and *Other Flowers of St. Francis*. His four-volume novel *Jezus z Nazaretu (Jesus of Nazareth, 1967-1973)* is deeply rooted in the daily practices and traditions of Judaism.

Justyna Braun holds a doctorate in comparative literature and has been teaching English at the Franciscan University of Steubenville since 2001.

Kazimierz Braun is a theater director, writer and theater historian. He has directed over 130 theater productions throughout Europe and the United States. His publications comprise more than thirty books in the field of theater history, including *A History of Polish Theatre* (in English and Polish), theater directing, fiction, drama and poetry. Since 1987, he has been teaching theater at the State University of New York at Buffalo. He and Justyna would also like to thank Zofia Reklewska-Braun, Father. Wladyslaw Meźyk, O.F.M. CONV., Dr. Stanislaw Cieślak, and Father Piotr Frankowski, O.F.M. CONV., for all their help.

Christopher Buckley was raised in Santa Barbara, California, and educated at St. Mary's College, San Diego State University, and the University of California Irvine. He has taught at Fresno State University, Murray State University, Kentucky, the University of California Santa Barbara, and West Chester University, Pennsylvania. He is professor and chair of the creative writing Department at the University of California Riverside. He has written eight books of poetry.

Scott Cairns is the author of five collections of poetry, most recently *Philokalia: New and Selected Poems*. His work has appeared in *The Paris Review, The New Republic, The Atlantic Monthly, Poetry, Image, Spiritus* and elsewhere. He serves as series editor for The Vassar Miller Prize in Poetry, and as professor of English at University of Missouri.

David Citino was born in Cleveland. He is the author of twelve volumes of poetry, most recently *The News and Other Poems* (University of Notre Dame Press), and *The Book of Appassionata: Collected Poems* and *The Invention of Secrecy* (both from Ohio State University Press). *Paperwork* (Kent State University Press), a collection of essays, appeared in 2004. He is a contributing editor of *The Eye of the Poet: Six Views of the Art and Craft of Poetry* (Oxford University Press) and teaches at Ohio State University.

William Bedford Clark is professor of English at Texas A&M University. He has published on a variety of topics in American literature and was founding editor of *The South Central Review*. His verse has appeared in *Christianity and Literature, Academic Questions, The Xavier Review* and *Southwestern American Literature*. He is presently at work on a multi-volume edition of Robert Penn Warren's letters.

Billy Collins was appointed Poet Laureate Consultant in Poetry. In 2002 he was appointed to a second term, continuing through 2003. Distinguished Professor of English at Lehman College, CUNY, he has written eight books of poetry, the most recent *Sailing Alone Around the Room* (2002). His many honors include an NEA Fellowship, the New York Foundation for the Arts Fellowship, the Levinson Prize and a Guggenheim Foundation Award.
Robert Cording's many publications include the books *What Binds Us to This World* (Copper Beech) and *Life-List* (Ohio State University Press). *Life-List* was the winner of the first Ohio State University Press/*The Journal* award. He

received an NEW Poetry Fellowship and a fellowship from the Connecticut Arts Commission for Poetry. He was poet in residence at The First Place in 1992.

Chet Corey is a Covenant Affiliate of the Franciscan Sisters of Perpetual Adoration (LaCrosse, Wisconsin). His poetry has appeared in a number of religious publications, including *National Catholic Reporter, St. Anthony Messenger, Ruah* and *Windhover*. He lives with his wife Kathy, a spiritual director, in Bloomington, Minnesota. He has directed retreats in writing poetry of the sacred at centers in Iowa, Minnesota and Wisconsin.

David Craig has been teaching creative writing at the Franciscan University of Steubenville for the last seventeen years. His most recent poetry collection is entitled *The Hive of the Saints* (2005).

Carlo Danese grew up in New Jersey and New York before attending North Carolina State University, where he majored in architecture but was drawn by poetry, literature and drama. He has traveled in Europe, North Africa, Latin America and the United States. He has worked in design and construction, sold Bic pens, driven yellow cabs, sweltered in the engine room of a transatlantic freighter and written poetry, plays and stories.

Jim Daniels is the author of eight books of poetry and two collections of short stories. His most recent books include *Show and Tell: New and Selected Poems* (University of Wisconsin Press) and *Detroit Tales* (Michigan State University Press) both published in 2003. He is the Thomas Baker Professor of English at Carnegie Mellon University in Pittsburgh.

Jacopone da Todi (c. 1230-1306) entered the Order of Friars Minor during the last part of the thirteenth century when the conflict between the Franciscan Conventuals and Spirituals was raging. His *Lauds*, which long have had an established place in the history of Italian poetry, sing the praises of poverty, insist on the supremacy of the love of God and inveigh against the worldliness of Pope Boniface VIII—a fact which would have pleased Dante to no end.

John F. Deane was born on Achill Island in 1943. He is the founder of *Poetry Ireland* and *The Poetry Ireland Review*. His latest book of poetry is *Manhandling the Deity*, (Carcanet Press, 2003), which was shortlisted for the T.S. Eliot Award. He also has The O'Shaughnessy Award, the Marten Toonder Award and the Ted McNulty Award, among others, to his credit. A member of Aosdana, the Irish Arts Academy, his *The Instruments of Art* is forthcoming from Carcanet Press.

Mark DeCarteret has published widely, most recently *Cream City Review, Conduit, Poetry East Mudlark* and *New American Poetry: The Next Generation* (Carnegie Mellon Press, 2000). He also has a new chapbook, *The Great Apology*, recently published by Oyster River Press.

Thomas Dorsett is a pediatrician who has published poetry in over four hundred journals. He is the author of *Dance Fire Dance* (Icarus, 1993) and a German translation, *Der Schlangenstock*, of Jim Wayne Miller's *Copperhead Cane* (Green River Writers, 1995), which is the translation of a recently discovered diary and poems written by a young Jewish girl in Nazi Germany.

Louise Erdrich draws her characters for novels and short stories from her experiences around the Turtle Mountain reservation. She is the author of *Love Medicine, Tracks, The Beet Queen, The Bingo Palace, Tales of Burning Love, The Last Report on the Miracles at Little No Horse* and *The Master Butcher's Singing Club*, as well as two books of poetry: *Baptism of Desire* and *Jacklight*. She also cowrote "Crown of Columbus" with Michael Dorris.

Marcene Gandolfo's poems have appeared recently in *The Paterson Literary Review, Earth's Daughters, Squaw Valley Review* and *Poetry Evolution*. She has taught writing at several Sacramento area colleges, and currently lives in Elk Grove, California, with her husband and daughter.

Jorie Graham has numerous books, including *Hybrids of Ghosts and Plants* and *Erosion*; a recent collection of poetry, *The Dream of the Unified Field: Selected Poems 1974-1994*, was published by The Ecco Press and was awarded the 1996 Pulitzer Prize in Poetry.

Seamus Heaney was born in 1939, at Mossbawn, thirty miles northwest of Belfast, in Northern Ireland. His first book, *Death of the Naturalist*, was published in 1966. Heaney is the author of thirteen collections of poetry, three volumes of criticism and other works. He is the Foreign Member of the American Academy of Arts and Letters and was Professor of Poetry at Oxford from 1989–1994. In 1995 he received the Nobel Prize in Literature. A resident of Dublin since 1976, he spends part of each year teaching at Harvard University, where he was elected the Boylston Professor of Rhetoric and Oratory in 1984.

Michael Heffernan has published six books of poetry, including an Iowa Poetry Prize selection (*Love's Answer*, 1994). His seventh book, *The Night Breeze off the Ocean*, is forthcoming in 2005 from Eastern Washington University Press. He's won three NEA grants in poetry and has seen his work appear in two Pushcart anthologies (XXII and XXV). He teaches in the M.F.A. program in creative writing at the University of Arkansas.

John Holmes wrote his series of Franciscan sonnets (which came out of the blue) some years ago as he was finishing up a dissertation on mysticism. He is a professor of English at the Franciscan University in Steubenville where he lives with his wife, Von, and their four sons. He counts Charles Brockden Brown and J.R.R. Tolkien as the subjects of much of his recent scholarly work.

David Brendan Hopes lives in Asheville, North Carolina, where he is professor of literature at the University of North Carolina and director of Urthona Press, the Black Swan Theater Company and the Downtown School of the Arts. Hopes earned a B.A. at Hiram College, an M.A. at Johns Hopkins University and an M.A. and Ph.D. at Syracuse University. His first collection, *The Glacier's Daughters*, won the Juniper Prize and the Saxfrage Prize. Gerard Manley Hopkins, 1844-1889, in 1864 first read John Henry Newman's *Apologia pro via sua*, which led to his decision to become a Catholic. Two years later, Newman himself received Hopkins into the Roman Catholic church. Hopkins soon decided to become a priest himself, and in 1867 he entered a Jesuit novitiate. Hopkins then destroyed all of the poetry he had written to date and would not write poems again until 1875, when his new work showed the flexibility and strength of the verse that would make him famous.

Andrew Hudgins has published five books of poetry with Houghton Mifflin: *Babylon in a Jar* (1998), *The Glass Hammer* (1995), *The Never-Ending* (1991), *After the Lost War* (1988) and *Saints and Strangers* (1985). A new collection, *Ecstatic in the Poison,* was published by The Overlook Press/Sewanee Writers' Series in 2003. He's also the author of a collection of literary essays, *The Glass Anvil*, which was published by the University of Michigan Press in 1997. *Saints and Strangers* was one of three finalists for the 1985 Pulitzer Prize in Poetry, *After the Lost War* received the Poets' Prize in 1989 and *The Never-Ending* was one of five finalists for the National Book Award in 1991. Hudgins is currently a Humanities Distinguished Professor in English at the Ohio State University.

Larry Janowski, O.F.M., has been a Franciscan friar (Assumption B.V.M. Province) since 1968. He is an adjunct professor of English at Wilbur Wright Community College in his native Chicago where he writes and performs his award-winning poetry. His M.F.A. is from Vermont College.

Mark Jarman is the author of numerous collections of poetry: *To the Green Man* (Consortium, 2004); *Unholy Sonnets* (2000); *Questions for Ecclesiastes*, which won the 1998 Lenore Marshall Poetry Prize and was a finalist for the National Book Critics Circle Award; *The Black Riviera* (1990), which won the 1991 Poets' Prize; *Far and Away* (1985); *The Rote Walker* (1981); and *North Sea* (1978). In 1992 he published *Iris*, a book-length poem.

Alexander Levering Kern is a poet and writer who lives in Somerville, Massachusetts; his poetry appears in *Quaker Life* and elsewhere, and other recent credits include *Boston Theological Institute Bulletin, Today's Minstry* and *Honduras Hope*. He teaches at Andover Newton Theological School.

Maurice Kilwein-Guevara was born in Belencito, Colombia, and raised in Pittsburgh, Pennsylvania. He is professor of English at the University of Wisconsin-Milwaukee. His books are *Postmortem, Poems of the River Spirit* and *Autobiography of So-and-So*.

Galway Kinnell was born in Providence, Rhode Island, on February 1, 1927. He grew up in Pawtucket, Rhode Island. After graduating from Princeton University, Kinnell went on to the University of Rochester, where he received his master's degree in English in 1949. After serving in the navy, he taught in many places, including Iran. He has won prizes for his translations of François Villon, Yves Bonnefoy and Rainer Maria Rilke and his own poetry has been translated into many languages.

Robert Kirschten is the author of *James Dickey and the Gentle Ecstasy of Earth* and *Ritual and the Shape of Myth in A.R. Ammons and James Dickey*, as well as several edited volumes and three collections of poetry. He holds a Ph.D. from the University of Chicago and is director of creative writing at Prairie View A&M University.

Steve Lautermilch is a poet and photographer who lives on the Outer Banks of North Carolina, where he leads workshops in dream study, meditation and writing. He recently spent time in the Southwest, camping and hiking in the back country, writing and making photographs for a show and study of Native American rock art. Born in Ohio, Steve has a Ph.D. in English from the University of Michigan. He taught writing and drama for twenty-one years at University of North Carolina-Greensboro. His chapbook of poems, *Triangle, Circle, Square*, won the 1998 *Ruah* competition.

Sydney Lea founded and for thirteen years edited *New England Review*. His books include a novel, *A Place in Mind*, two collections of naturalist nonfiction, *Hunting the Whole Way Home* and *A Little Wildness*, and eight collections of poetry. *Pursuit of a Wound* (2000) was a finalist for the Pulitzer Prize and *To the Bone* won the 1998 Poets' Prize. His latest book of verse is *Ghost Rain* (Sarabande Books).

Denise Levertov was born in Ilford, England, in 1923. She published her first piece of poetry at the age of seventeen in *Poetry Quarterly*. In her youth, Levertov spent three years in London working as a nurse with World War II veterans. After work hours, she wrote poetry. Eventually she married and moved to the United States, where she became associated with the Black Mountain poets: Creeley, Olson and Duncan. In her late thirties and early forties she was the editor of *The Nation* (1961, 1963–1965), and received national recognition for her poetry, namely by being awarded the Lenore Marshall Poetry Prize. Always politically active, especially during the Vietnam War, Levertov's work became more and more overtly spiritual as she moved through her years. She died in 1997.

Jerzy Liebert, 1904–1931, was born to a Jewish family and converted to Catholicism at the University of Warsaw, where he studied Polish literature. Liebert made his debut in *Skamander*, an influential, avant-garde literary journal. He became especially known for his lyric poetry, often revolving around his religious experiences.

Vachel Lindsay, 1879–1931, American poet, was born in Springfield, Illinois, studied at Hiram College, the Art Institute of Chicago and the New York School of Art. He toured around the country selling his art and his muscular, rhythmic poetry. Volumes of his poetry include *General William Booth Enters into Heaven* (1913), *The Congo* (1914), *The Chinese Nightingale* (1917) and *Collected Poems* (1938).

Herbert Lomas is a poet, translator and regular critic for *London Magazine*, *Ambit* and other journals. Of his ten books of poetry, *The Vale of Todmorden* (Arc, 2003) is the most recent. His *Letters in the Dark* was an *Observer* book of the year, and he has received Guinness, Arvon and Cholmondely awards. He has translated thirteen books of poetry and prose and is a regular translator for *Books from Finland*. His *Contemporary Finnish Poetry* won the Poetry Society's 1991 biennial translation award. He is a member of the Finnish Academy, and he was made Knight First Class, Order of the White Rose of Finland "for his services to Finnish Literature." A former Senior Lecturer at the University of Helsinki and Principal Lecturer at the University of London, he lives in Aldeburgh, Suffolk, England.

Michael H. Lythgoe was educated at St. Louis University and the University of Notre Dame. After retiring as an Air Force officer, he also earned the M.F.A. from Bennington College. His poems, interviews and reviews have appeared in *Christianity and Literature, The Caribbean Writer, The Writer's Chronicle, Windhover, Aries, Yemasee, Praesidium* and *Moveo Angelus*. He and his wife reside in Aiken, South Carolina.

Marjorie Maddox has one full-length book and five chapbooks to her credit. She has, as well, published over 260 poems and short stories in journals and has won many awards, too numerous to mention here.

Leo Luke Marcello got his advanced degrees from Louisiana State University and is the author of four books of poetry. The winner of many awards, he taught in the Department of Languages of McNeese State University until his untimely death in 2005.

William Matthews, 1942–1997, was a popular and prolific poet. During his lifetime he published eleven books of poetry, including *Time & Money* (1996), which won the National Book Critics Circle Award and was a finalist for the Lenore Marshall Poetry Prize; *Selected Poems and Translations 1969–1991* (1992); *Blues If You Want* (1989); *A Happy Childhood* (1984); *Rising and Falling* (1979); *Sticks and Stones* (1975); and *Ruining the New Road* (1970).

Janet McCann is a Texas poet who has been teaching at Texas A&M for thirty-five years. Her most recent collection is *Pascal Goes to the Races* (2004).

Phyllis McGinley, 1905–1978, known for her light verse, treats aspects of her culture with humor and underlying seriousness. Her best-known collections of verse include *A Pocketful of Wry* (1940), *The Love Letters of Phyllis McGinley* (1950) and *Times Three* (1960); *Saint-Watching* (1969) recounts the lives of various saints (through her wry lenses).

Father Thomas Merton is perhaps the most well known of all American Catholic poets this century. From (mostly) his Abbey at Gethsemani, Kentucky, Merton wrote volumes of poetry, social criticism and contemplative distillations for New Directions and other presses.

Gabriela Mistral (1889–1957), pseudonym for Lucila Godoy y Alcayaga, was born in Vicuña, Chile. She was a poet and social activist who affected education reform. Her complete poetry was published in 1958. Mistral, a member of the Third Order Franciscans, won the Nobel Prize for Literature in 1945.

Howard Moss was a poet, critic, dramatist and editor. Born in 1922 in New York, Moss was a lifelong New Yorker who was poetry editor of *The New Yorker* magazine for over three decades, until his death in 1987. He received the National Book Award for poetry for his *Selected Poems* in 1971.

Kay Mullen lives on the Olympic Peninsula with her husband. She is a former teacher and elementary school counselor, currently a licensed mental health counselor. Her work has appeared in Appalachia, PoetsWest, Minotaur, New Works Review, White Heron Press, Pontoon Anthology, Tamaphyr Mountain Poetry and others. Her first book of poems, Let Morning Begin, was published in 2001 by Caritas Communications, Mequon, Wisconsin.

Marilyn Nelson is professor of English at the University of Connecticut. Her third book won the Annisfield-Wolf Award and was a finalist for the National Book Award; her fifth book was a finalist for the National Book Award, the PEN/Winship Award and the Lenore Marshall Poetry Prize, and won the 1999 Poets' Prize; her sixth book, *Carver: A Life in Poems,* by Front Street Books, won the Boston Globe/Hornbook Award, was a finalist for the National Book Award, was a Newbery Honor Book and won the Flora Stieglitz Straus Award. In 2002 she became poet laureate of the State of Connecticut.

Daniel Nodes is chairman of classics at Ave Maria University, Naples, Florida. Dr. Nodes has published two books on Christian Latin poetry and frequently writes on the Church Fathers. He holds the Ph.D. from the University of Toronto.

Roger Pfingston was born and raised in Evansville, Indiana, where he later went to Indiana University, graduating in 1962. He taught high school in Bloomington, Indiana, from 1967 until his retirement in 1997. Pfingston's work has appeared recently in *2River View, For Poetry, In Posse, The Adirondack Review* and in recent print issues of *Poet Lore, Wisconsin Review, Rhino, WordWright* and *The Sow's Ear Poetry Review.*

Kenneth Rexroth, poet and translator, was born in South Bend, Indiana. After his expulsion from high school, he educated himself in lecture halls and hobo camps while working as a wrestler, soda jerk, clerk and reporter. In 1923 and 1924 he served a prison term for partial ownership of a brothel. As a youth he backpacked across the country and spent two months in a monastery. During the '30s he studied mysticism—Boehme, Aquinas and Scotus—and Communism, becoming a pacifist. During the Second World War he registered as a conscientious objector and served as a psychiatric orderly. In the late '40s he became the center and poetic father of the

evolving Beat scene in and around San Francisco. His work was later domi-
nated by Eastern philosophy, and he continued being a valued presence to
many young poets. Characteristically, at his funeral, Catholic eulogies,
Buddhist chants and Beat poems were performed.

James Miller Robinson has had recent or will have upcoming poems in
*Mochila Review, Mid-American Poetry Review, Spirit Literature, Kaleidoscope,
GW Review* and others. He teaches Spanish at Huntsville High School and at
the University of Alabama in Huntsville, Alabama.

Dante Gabriel Rossetti, born in 1828, was a painter and a poet, one of the
founding members of the Pre-Raphaelites. He probably started to write his
poetry while attending Royal Academy, wanting to write poetry which rejected
Victorian materialism, which would bring back into art a pre-Renaissance
purity of style and spirit. After his wife died of an overdose of laudanum in
1862, Rossetti buried with her the only complete manuscript of his poems.
The manuscript was recovered seven years later and published in 1870.
Though shadowed by health problems in his later years, he was admired by a
younger generation of aesthetes such as Oscar Wilde.

Helen Ruggieri lives in Olean, New York, and attended St. Bonaventure
University. She has had work in the anthology *Place of Passage*, and recently
in *Spoon River Poetry Review, Cream City Review* and *Portraits*. A book of
Haibun, *The Character for Spirit*, is available from foothillspublishing.com.

Luci Shaw is a poet, essayist, teacher and retreat leader. Author of a number
of prose books and eight volumes of poetry, including *Writing the River, The
Angles of Light, The Green Earth* and *Water Lines*, she is writer in residence at
Regent College, Vancouver, Canada, and lives in Bellingham, Washington.
Her new book on the adventure with God, forthcoming from InterVarsity
Press, is *The Crime of Living Cautiously*.

Olympia Sibley is a nontraditional doctoral candidate at Texas A&M
University. She has one husband, three daughters and a pit-bull. Her areas of
interest include FWW era poetry, so-called "domestic women's poetry," the
modernist long poem and novels-in-verse.

David St. John was born in Fresno, California, in 1949. St. John received an
M.F.A. in 1974 from the University of Iowa. He is the author of six books
of poetry, including *Prism* (Arctos Press, 2002), *Study for the World's Body:
New and Selected Poems* (1994), *No Heaven* (1985) and *Hush* (1976). His
awards include the Discover/*The Nation* prize, the James D. Phelan Prize and

the prix de Rome fellowship in literature, several National Endowment for the Arts Fellowships and a Guggenheim Fellowship. He teaches at the University of Southern California, Los Angeles.

Kim Stafford directs the William Stafford Center at Lewis & Clark College in Oregon. He is the author of *Early Morning* (Graywolf Press, 2002) and *The Muses Among Us: Eloquent Listening and other Pleasures of the Writer's Craft* (University of Georgia Press, 2003).

Sue Standing's most recent collection of poems is *False Horizon* (Four Way Books, 2003). She teaches creative writing and African literature at Wheaton College in Norton, Massachusetts.

Alfred Lord Tennyson, 1809–1892, was an English poet who is often regarded as the chief representative of the Victorian age in poetry, succeeding Wordsworth as Poet Laureate in 1850. He studied at Trinity College, Cambridge, where he joined the literary club, "The Apostles," and met Arthur Hallam, who became his closest friend and whom he would immortalize in his *In Memoriam*. He later published his *Idylls of the King*, dealing with the Arthurian theme, in 1885, and is buried in the Poets' Corner in Westminster Abbey.

Francis Thompson, 1859–1907, was part of what is often called the Catholic Renaissance in England. He rebelled against his father, who wanted him to become a doctor, and took to wandering the London streets, selling matches and hailing cabs for money, becoming addicted to opium. Having sent poems to a new Catholic magazine, *Merry England*, Francis was rescued by its editor Mr. Wilfrid Meynell and his wife, the poet Alice Meynell, who helped him get set up for a time at a monastery. The two of them finally helped Francis find more permanent settlement near them in London, where he was either an intimate or a constant visitor until his death nineteen years later. He is best known for his "The Hound of Heaven."

Eric Trethewey has published five books of poems, most recently *Songs and Lamentations*. His poems, stories, essays and reviews have appeared in numerous magazines and anthologies in the United States, Canada and Britain, among them *The Atlantic Monthly*, *The Georgia Review*, the *Kenyon Review*, *The Paris Review* and *Poetry*.

Jan Twardowski, born in 1915, is a Roman Catholic priest and poet. As a member of the underground in the Polish Home Army (AK) during WWII, Father Twardowski took part in the Warsaw uprising in 1944. He was wounded and permanently handicapped. Father Twardowski has published several volumes of poetry. His works appear regularly in anthologies of contemporary Polish verse and are well known among critics, amateurs and students. His poems, often distinguished by their warmth and wit, express unceasing admiration for the Creator, whose image can be found in the smallest aspects of nature.

Evelyn Underhill was born in 1850 and grew up in London. Her friends included Laurence Housman (poet and brother of the poet A.E. Housman), Sarah Bernhardt and Baron Friedrich von Huegel, a writer on theology and mysticism. Largely under his guidance, she embarked on a life of reading, writing, meditation and prayer. From her studies and experience she produced poetry and a series of books on contemplative prayer. She believed that contemplative prayer was for everyone and insisted that modern psychological theory could be used to enhance that experience. In her later years, she spent a great deal of time as a lecturer and retreat director. She died in 1941.

Sean Webb's work has appeared in *North American Review, Prairie Schooner, Nimrod* and many other publications. He has been the recipient of numerous awards and honors; most recently he won the Philadelphia City Paper annual writing contest.

William Carlos Williams, 1883–1963, was one of the major Modernist poets. A friend of Pound and a pediatrician by trade, he, like Stevens and Moore, decided to stay home in America and, in his case, write a more local poetry. He detested Eliot's obsession with European culture and waged a one-sided battle against his influence for most of his writing life. Later, he became a kind of father figure for the Beats and other postmodernist writers. Besides leaving his long poem *Patterson* behind, he bequeathed to his readers a wonderful collection of lyrical work, which includes some of the finest poetry on the poor in our language.

Brother Rick Wilson (Brother Didacus), T.O.R., is a Franciscan friar in the Immaculate Conception Province. Born in a military family in Verdun, France, he has degrees from George Mason University and a doctorate from The Catholic University. He has also trained at St. Elizabeth's Hospital for two years in the bibliotherapy program and is seeking to become a registered poetry therapist. His dissertation was on the mysticism in the poetry of James Wright. He is the author of two   collections of poetry and his poems have appeared in over one hundred publications.

Józef Wittlin,1896–1976, was a poet, novelist, translator and literary critic. Wittlin studied philosophy and languages at the University of Vienna. He served as a soldier in the First World War. After the war, he continued his studies in Lviv. He became a member of the influential literary movement affiliated with the journal *Skamander*. His achievements include an acclaimed translation of the *Odyssey* into Polish and a novel, *Sól ziemi (Salt of the Earth)*, which has been translated into several European languages. Between 1925 and 1926, Wittlin lived in Assisi, where he worked on a book about Saint Francis. At the outbreak of WWII in 1939, Wittlin became an exile in France and Portugal. In 1941 he sailed for the United States, where he remained for the rest of his life. He collaborated with Radio Free Europe, published a Polish weekly (*Tygodnik Polski*) in New York, and authored several volumes of essays, translations and memoirs. Wittlin's poems were known for their pacifist themes. He was influenced by German expressionism, but also drew on the traditions of the Renaissance and the Baroque.

William Wordsworth, 1770–1850, British poet, was credited with ushering in the English Romantic Movement with the publication of *Lyrical Ballads*, 1789, in collaboration with Samuel Taylor Coleridge. He became a Christian and England's poet laureate late in life. Though much of his late conservative work is beautiful, in general it has left critics cold.

Charles Wright was born in Pickwick Dam, Tennessee, in 1935 and was educated at Davidson College and the University of Iowa. *Chickamauga*, his eleventh collection of poems, won the 1996 Lenore Marshall Poetry Prize. His other books include *Buffalo Yoga* (Farrar, Straus & Giroux, 2004); *Negative Blue* (2000); *Appalachia* (1998); *Black Zodiac* (1997), which won the Pulitzer Prize and the *Los Angeles Times* Book Prize; *The World of the Ten Thousand Things: Poems 1980–1990*; *Zone Journals* (1988); *Country Music: Selected Early Poems* (1983), which won the National Book Award; *Hard Freight* (1973), which was nominated for the National Book Award; and two volumes of criticism: *Halflife* (1988) and *Quarter Notes* (1995). His translation of Eugenio Montale's *The Storm and Other Poems* (1978) was awarded the PEN Translation Prize. His many honors include the American Academy of Arts and Letters Award of Merit Medal and the Ruth Lilly Poetry Prize. In 1999 he was elected a Chancellor of The Academy of American Poets. He is Souder Family Professor of English at the University of Virginia in Charlottesville.

Saint Clare of Assisi was born in 1194 and died in 1253. "The Fourth Letter to Blessed Agnes of Prague," as well as other information about her life and writings can be found in *Clare of Assisi: Early Documents*, Regis J. Armstrong, trans. (New York: The Franciscan Institute, 1993).

Saint Francis of Assisi was born around 1181 and died in 1226. "The Canticle of Creatures" and Francis' other writings and life works can be found in *Francis of Assisi: Early Documents*, Volume I–III, Regis J. Armstrong, J.A. Wayne Hellmann and William J. Short, eds. (New York: New City Press, 1999).

Acknowledgments

Note: This anthology is to benefit Catholic Charities; most poets and editors have donated their royalties and permissions fees to help in the effort to relieve hunger and misery throughout the world. We are grateful for the donation of the use of these fine poems.

The editors would first of all like to thank Father Murray Bodo, both for his introduction and for his little anthology, *ClareSong* (Ottocentro Press) which proved a great starting point for this collection.

Aligheri, Dante: Sections from both the *Inferno* and *Paradiso* were taken from Henry Wadsworth Longfellow's translation (1865 and 1867), Houghton, Mifflin & Co (1893 and 1895).

Jan Lee Ande's poem is reprinted by permission of the author. "The Annunciation of Francis" first appeared in her book, *Reliquary*, published by Texas Review Press, 2003.

Anonymous: "Legenda versificata sanctae Clarae: How Clare, converted from the world by Francis' influence, entered the religious life (1212 A.D.)," edited by G. Cremascoli, *in Fontes Franciscani, a. c. di E. Menestro, S. Brufani et alii, Edizioni Porziuncola*, 1995, pp. 2347–2399, translated by Daniel J. Nodes.

Bodo, Murray: *"The Letters of Clare to Agnes of Prague," "The Rooms of St. Clare," "St. Clare Dies at her Mirror," "Directions for Pilgrims"* and *"St. Clare— Summer Night, Scattered Clouds"* appeared in *Icarus in Assisi*, Editrice Minerva Assisi, Vicolo degli Arch I – 06081 Assisi, 2002.

John Bowers's poem is published by permission of the author.

Roman Brandstaetter's poem is published by permission of his estate.

Buckley, Christopher. "Giotto's 'St. Francis Preaching to the Birds'" appeared in *Blue Autumn*. Copyright 1990, Copper Beach Press. Poem is published by permission of the author.
Scott Cairns's poem is published by permission of the author.

Citino, David. "Francis Meets a Leper" appeared in *The Gift of Fire*. Permission to reprint is granted by the author.

William Bedford Clark's poem is published by permission of the author.

Billy Collins's poem is reprinted by permission of the author. It first appeared in *Five Points*.

Robert Cording: "Assisi" from *What Binds Us to This World*, © 1991 by Robert Cording, Copper Beech Press, English Dept., Box 1852, Brown University, Providence, RI 02912.

Chet Corey's poem is published by permission of the author.

David Craig's poems are published by permission of the author. "Chapter One," "Chapter Two" and "Chapter Three," also appear in *The Hive of the Saints*, copyright © 2005 by David Craig, iUniverse Press, New York.

Carlo Danese's poem is published by permission of the author.

Daniels, Jim. "Niagara Falls" appeared in *Show and Tell*. Copyright 2003. Reprinted by permission of The University of Wisconsin Press.

Excerpts from *Jacapone da Todi: The Lauds* were translated by Serge and Elizabeth Hughes, introduction by Serge Hughes, preface by Elemire Zolla, Copyright ©1982 by Paulist Press, Inc., New York/Mahwah, N.J. Used with permission of Paulist Press. www.paulistpress.com

Deane, John F.: "The Poor Ladies of San Damiano" and "Francis of Assisi 1182:1982" from *The Stylized City, New and Selected Poems*, The Daedalus Press, Dublin, 1991, is reprinted with permission of the poet and publisher.

Mark DeCarteret's poem is published by permission of the author.

Thomas Dorsett's poems are published by the permission of the author.

"Saint Clare" from *Baptism of Desire* by Louise Erdrich. Copyright © 1990 by Louise Erdrich. Reprinted by permission of HarperCollins Publishers Inc.

Marcene Gandolfo's poem is published by permission of the author.

Graham, Jorie: "At the Exhumed Body of Santa Clara, Assisi," from *Erosion*, 1983, is reprinted with permission of Princeton University Press.

"Saint Francis and the Birds" from *Death of a Naturalist* by Seamus Heaney published by Faber and Faber Ltd. Used by permission of the publisher.

Michael Heffernan's poem is published by permission of the author.

Holmes, John: "Solvite Templum Hoc" was first published in *The Cord* 38 (1988), 159, and then reprinted in *Odd Angles of Heaven* (1994).

Hopes, David Brendan: "Leo, Little Brother Lamb of God, to Lady Chastity," was published in *Bennington Review*, #3 Dec. 1978, p. 30,   *The Literary*

Review, Vol XXX, #4, summer, 1987, p. 553, and in *The Penitent Magdalene*, Franciscan University of Steubenville Press, 1992.

Hudgins, Andrew: "Fire and St. Francis," from *Saints and Strangers* by Andrew Hudgins. Copyright © 1985 by Andrew Hudgins. Reprinted by permission of Houghton Mifflin Company. All rights reserved.

Janowski, Father Larry, O.F.M.: "The Lady Clare Sees St. Francis Naked" was published in *Celibate Dazzled*, Franciscan University of Steubenville Press, 2003.

Jarman, Mark: "Testimony of a Roasted Chicken" is reprinted from *To the Green Man by Mark Jarman*, published by Sarabande Books, Inc. Copyright © 2004 by Mark Jarman. Reprinted by permission of Sarabande Books and the author.

Alexander Levering Kern's poem is published by permission of the author.

Maurice Kilwein-Guevara's poem is published by permission of the author.

Kinnell, Galway: "St. Francis and the Sow," from *Mortal Acts, Mortal Words* by Galway Kinnell. Copyright © 1980 by Galway Kinnell. Reprinted by permission of Houghton Mifflin Company. All rights reserved.

Robert Kirschten: "Aunt Til" originally appeared in *Old Family Movies*.

Lautermilch, Steve: "After a Dream of Clare and Francis of Assisi" appeared in *Image* 59 (January 1996), 44.
Lea, Sydney: "Transport" appeared in *Christian Century*, Winter 2004.

Levertov, Denise: "Brother Ivy," from *Evening Train*, copyright © 1992 by Denise Levertov. Reprinted by permission of New Directions Publishing Corp.

Lomas, Herbert: "Assisi and Back," appeared in *The Hudson Review*, Vol. XLI, No. 3, Autumn, 1988. Reprinted with permission of the poet and *The Hudson Review*.

Michael Lythgoe's poem is published by permission of the author.

Marjorie Maddox's poem is published by permission of the author.

Leo Luke Marcello's poem is published by permission of the author.

Topical Index

INDEX OF FIRST LINES